Queer Legacies

Queer Legacies

Stories from Chicago's LGBTQ Archives

John D'Emilio

The University of Chicago Press

Chicago and London

The University of Chicago Press, Chicago 60637
The University of Chicago Press, Ltd., London
© 2020 by The University of Chicago
Published 2020
Printed in the United States of America

29 28 27 26 25 24 23 22 21 20   1 2 3 4 5

ISBN-13: 978-0-226-66497-2 (cloth)
ISBN-13: 978-0-226-72753-0 (paper)
ISBN-13: 978-0-226-72767-7 (e-book)
DOI: https://doi.org/10.7208/chicago/9780226727677.001
.0001

Library of Congress Cataloging-in-Publication Data

Names: D'Emilio, John, author. | Gerber/Hart Library and
    Archives.
Title: Queer legacies : stories from Chicago's LGBTQ
    archives / John D'Emilio.
Description: Chicago ; London : The University of Chicago
    Press, 2020. | Includes bibliographical references and
    index.
Identifiers: LCCN 2019058293 | ISBN 9780226664972
    (cloth) | ISBN 9780226727530 (paperback) |
    ISBN 9780226727677 (ebook)
Subjects: LCSH: Gays—Illinois—Chicago—History. | Sexual
    minority community—Illinois—Chicago. | Gays—Illinois—
    Chicago—Societies, etc. | Gay liberation movement—
    Illinois—Chicago. | Chicago (Ill.)—History—20th century.
Classification: LCC HQ76.3.U52 I444 2020 | DDC
    306.76/60977311—dc23
LC record available at https://lccn.loc.gov/2019058293

♾ This paper meets the requirements of ANSI/NISO
Z39.48-1992 (Permanence of Paper).

Dedicated to the memory of Gregory Sprague
(1951–1987), a pioneer

Contents

Introduction

In 1969, when the Stonewall Rebellion in New York gave birth to what was then described as the gay liberation movement, a core part of the oppression that activists fought was invisibility. The theme surfaced in almost all the work that activists did. Being visible was understood as a critical component of the fight against oppression. "Come Out! Come Out!" was one of the most common slogans shouted at demonstrations and expressed in the writings of activists. *Come Out!* was the name of the first post-Stonewall publication produced by activists in New York. By coming out, LGBTQ people would find each other and build community. Visibility throughout society and its institutions would dispel the myths and stereotypes that the heterosexual majority held and that sustained institutionalized homophobia.

In the decade that followed, only a small proportion of the LGBTQ population came out. The cost of visibility was still too high. When the AIDS epidemic struck and quickly spread in the 1980s and early 1990s, the vast majority were still in the closet. Mainstream media continued to propagate negative views of same-sex love and gender nonconformity, and it largely ignored the work of activists.

By contrast, today, in the third decade of the twenty-first century, LGBTQ people—lesbian, gay, bisexual, transgender, and queer/questioning—have achieved a level of visibility in politics, culture, and daily life beyond anything that was even imaginable half a century ago. A white gay man seeks the Democratic nomination for president, and his campaign is taken seriously by political pundits. A black lesbian is elected mayor of Chicago. A television series about a parent who is in the process of gender transition is a success with critics and the public. A film about a black gay teenager wins the Oscar for Best Picture. Wedding announcements in which both spouses are of the same gender regularly appear in our newspapers. Hundreds of the nation's largest corporations recognize and support LGBTQ employee groups. The positive change that has occurred in the fifty-plus years since Stonewall, though still incomplete and unevenly distributed, is deep and profound.

There remains, however, at least one important area of life where invisibility remains more common than not. For many years, I had the privilege of teaching courses on LGBTQ issues and history at the University of Illinois at Chicago. The classes drew a wide range of students across the sexual and gender spectrum as well as across racial, ethnic, and religious identities. And yet across those differences, one commonality stood out. Except for a very small number of self-defined "queer" activists, few of the students knew anything about LGBTQ history. Many had gone to high schools with Gay-Straight Alliances, but yet had never heard a word about LGBTQ history in the classroom. Many went each June to watch Chicago's massive Pride Parade, an annual event commemorating the 1969 uprising at the Stonewall Inn, but they were not aware of the reason for the parade.

The irony in this continuing invisibility of a community's and a movement's history is immense. An important component of the activism of the 1970s and early 1980s was an effort to uncover, preserve, and present to the public a previously unknown and hidden history of LGBTQ life and culture. In the early 1970s, Jonathan Ned Katz began a search for evidence of a queer history. He wrote a play, *Coming Out*, that was staged in New York and elsewhere. It consisted of stories from the LGBTQ past in which the dialogue was drawn entirely from historical documents that Katz had uncovered. In 1976, he published *Gay American History*, a massive anthology of documents that stretched across four centuries of LGBTQ experience. Within just a few years, historians such as John Boswell and Lillian Faderman had published books that covered broad swaths of LGBTQ history and that received a great deal of public attention.[1]

In 1974, Joan Nestle and Deborah Edel, along with several others, founded the Lesbian Herstory Archives in New York, to my knowledge the first such effort at deliberate historic preservation.[2] The founders of the LHA made it their mission to spread the message that preserving the records of our history was a critical part of our liberation struggle. In the 1970s and 1980s, core members like Nestle and Edel traveled widely, giving public presentations meant to inspire and energize audiences to save their community's history. The impulse to create community history projects and archives spread quickly. By the end of the 1970s, such projects were underway in Los Angeles, San Francisco, Chicago, Boston, and elsewhere. Today, there are several dozen history projects and archival efforts in communities across the United States, and many mainstream institutions have joined the effort.

To me, this is all very exciting and hopeful. In 1974, when I began the research for what became my first book on LGBTQ history, *Sexual Politics, Sexual Communities*, except for a short visit to the Institute for Sex Research (commonly known as the Kinsey Institute), none of my research was conducted in archives.[3] Instead, I visited the homes of activists and worked my way through file cabinets and

1. Jonathan Ned Katz, *Gay American History: Lesbians and Gay Men in the U.S.A.* (New York: Thomas Crowell, 1976); John Boswell, *Christianity, Social Tolerance, and Homosexuality: Gay People in Western Europe from the Beginning of the Christian Era to the Fourteenth Century* (Chicago: University of Chicago Press, 1980); Lillian Faderman, *Surpassing the Love of Men: Romantic Friendship and Love between Women from the Renaissance to the Present* (New York: William Morrow, 1981).

2. See www.lesbianherstoryarchives.org.

3. John D'Emilio, *Sexual Politics, Sexual Communities: The Making of a Homosexual Minority in the United States, 1940-1970* (Chicago: University of Chicago Press, 1983).

boxes that they kept in their studies, living rooms, basements, and garages. I visited the offices of the early activist groups that still existed and explored their organizational records. In the case of the New York Mattachine Society, I was told one day that it would be closing at the end of the month and that I was welcome to take their office files home if it would be useful to me. I responded affirmatively, and for the next several years two four-drawer file cabinets of Mattachine records filled one of the closets in my apartment. The story is a reminder of how tenuous the survival of LGBTQ history can be.

The importance of preserving and archiving queer history was brought home to me in 2019. Throughout the United States, and indeed around the globe, tens of millions of people commemorated the fiftieth anniversary of the Stonewall Uprising. Stonewall is, without question, the best-known event in LGBTQ history. It has enough resonance with a significant segment of the public that Barack Obama was able to invoke it in his second inaugural address when he used the phrase "Seneca Falls, Selma, and Stonewall."

But how did we get to Stonewall? How many of us know that there were years of activism prior to Stonewall that helped create that moment? And, even more importantly, how did we get from Stonewall to where we are today, more than fifty years later? The vast changes that have occurred in politics and the law, in media, popular culture and the arts, and in social life and community have not happened magically. They did not occur simply because of several nights of rioting in New York in the early summer of 1969. They happened because of decisions made and actions taken by countless numbers of brave individuals throughout the United States.

The Stonewall fiftieth anniversary celebrations in 2019 spurred a growing interest in knowing more about this still largely hidden history. Some states, such as California and Illinois, have begun to mandate the inclusion of LGBTQ history in the curriculum. The Chicago Metro History Fair offers a prize for the best student paper on an LGBTQ topic, while the Organization of American Historians has an award for the best dissertation in the field. Podcasts like

Teaching Tolerance and websites like Outhistory are springing up in an effort to make sure this history has a vibrant presence on the web. These initiatives, along with others, are a welcome effort to make researching, teaching, and learning LGBTQ history far more widespread than is currently the case.[4]

With this volume, I hope to contribute to this endeavor. Through the story that each chapter tells, I attempt to shed light on some of the wide range of actions, experiences, and lives that have helped create a contemporary world in which there is a much greater degree of visibility and acceptance of LGBTQ people than was true at the time of the Stonewall Uprising. Most of the stories have a Chicago focus, a city often ignored in the broad narrative of LGBTQ history. Some focus on individuals, on their experiences of coming out and engaging in public activism. Some revolve around organizations and the collective effort to make change. Some are about particular events that had an impact on people and institutions. Some focus on political activism, some on community building, some on culture and the arts.

While each of the stories can be read on its own, at various points I make links between essays that have overlapping themes or content. When read together, I hope that they provide a deeper sense of the far-reaching changes that have occurred over the last several decades. Cumulatively, the actions of a wide range of "ordinary" individuals have made a big difference in the lives of many people and in society as a whole.

In the broadest sense, one could argue that all of these stories fall under the umbrella of what we might consider a movement for social change. Typically, social movements are understood only in terms of protest, organizing, and engagement with politics. Activists conduct voter registration drives; they endorse candidates and sometimes run for office themselves; they form picket lines; they organize marches; they occupy buildings and disrupt business as

4. See www.tolerance.org/podcasts/queer-america and www .outhistory.org.

usual; they protest in the street and block the flow of traffic. Without question, these are all core components of a movement challenging institutionalized inequality and injustice. But a successful movement, and especially one based on identifying with a group that is targeted for oppression, requires a range of methods for drawing people together. Efforts to build community ties through activities as diverse as athletics and musical performances have the effect of strengthening the foundations upon which a movement for justice is then able to stand. Cumulatively, I hope the essays in this volume lead to a more subtle and complicated understanding of how change happens and what might be considered activist or movement work.

Something that all of these stories have in common is that each emerges from a collection of documents at the Gerber/Hart Library and Archives. Founded in 1981 by Gregory Sprague, then a graduate student in history, and a few other Chicago activists, Gerber/Hart was an outgrowth of a community-based gay and lesbian history project. Operating on a thin budget and with the devotion of many volunteers, Gerber/Hart has been collecting and preserving the raw materials of Chicago's, and the Midwest's, LGBTQ history for four decades.[5] To most readers, the names of its archival collections—the Dennis Halan Collection, the Robinn Dupree Collection, the BEHIV Collection, the Melissa Ann Merry Collection—will mean nothing. But working my way through a large number of these collections, I found that each one contained valuable nuggets of the past. Each brings to life a moment or episode in the struggle against homophobia. Each tells a story, mostly forgotten and often surprising, of courage, resilience, and resistance to oppression. Each has the power to enlighten us about history and about how change happens.

My hope is that encountering these historical episodes will also accomplish another goal beyond absorbing the content of LGBTQ history. As I tell these stories, I also try to make visible the process of discovery. Historical research can seem remote, an activity that only a trained professional can do. But the archives of an institution

5. See www.gerberhart.org.

like Gerber/Hart—and others across the United States—are meant to be a resource for the communities that house and sustain them. Making one's way through the folders in a box of documents from more than a generation ago can provoke surprise, shock, excitement, laughter, and more. It can make the proverbial "lightbulb" go on as one finds a document that, suddenly, seems to create a deeper understanding than one had just a few minutes earlier. And the joy of discovering these unknown facts and episodes from the past can serve as a powerful reminder that LGBTQ history—and many other kinds of history as well—will come down to future generations only because of the many individuals who had the good sense to preserve the evidence of the past and because of those who then choose to explore that evidence and write about it.

The essays in this volume do not comprise the full sweep and scope of Chicago's LGBTQ history across the half century since Stonewall. Each one emerges from research in a particular collection at Gerber/Hart. Without question, there is more that can be discovered about each of these stories and more that can be told about Chicago's LGBTQ past. But, besides the revelations they provide about how we have moved from a pre-Stonewall world of the most intense oppression to one in which many, though not all, of us experience a great deal more freedom, I hope they also suggest the value of preserving historical records. There are many more stories from the past worth sharing, many more stories that deserve to be told and that we can all learn from.

1

Merle's Story

Our life stories are the core content of LGBTQ history. Yes, our organizations and businesses produce records that detail important work. And mainstream institutions and social structures affect us deeply. But the texture and the challenges of what it means to be lesbian, gay, bisexual, or transgender at different times and in different places will only fully emerge if we make an effort to collect a broad range of our life stories. Reading—or hearing—the life story of an individual is not only compelling and absorbing in its own right. It can also open doors of understanding and offer revealing insights into what it was like to be . . . well, whatever combination of identities the individual brings to the interview. Each of our life stories will have something to tell us beyond the L, G, B, T, or Q. We are also the products of regional culture, of racial and ethnic identity, of religious upbringing, of our particular family life, of class background, of work environments, and other matters as well.

Interviews—or "oral histories"—have been a key feature of the effort to recover an LGBTQ past. In the 1970s, when I began researching the history of activism before Stonewall, I conducted about two dozen interviews, often lasting several hours, with activists from the 1940s, '50s, and '60s. In Chicago, Gregory Sprague, one of the founders of the Gerber/Hart Library, along with other members of Chicago's Gay and Lesbian History Project, began conducting inter-

The interview can be found in the Jack Rinella Papers, Gerber/Hart Library and Archives.

views with Chicagoans in the late 1970s. They are a rich source of Chicago's queer history. One of them immediately captured my attention, because it told a story unlike any that I had heard before. Here is Merle's story, as she told it to Marjorie Miller in 1981.

* * *

Merle Markland was born in 1902 into a working-class family in Cuba, Illinois, a small downstate mining community. She had an older brother and two younger half brothers and a stepdad whom she loved dearly. Growing up, she recalled, "I'd never heard of the word lesbian or gay. I didn't know what that meant. I just knew I was different."

She played baseball with her brothers and "aggravated" them because "I'd be better than they were." From an early age, she "had a feeling for little girls." She wanted to walk them home from school and hold their hands and look after them. "I knew there was something wrong, but that was my secret. I didn't know what it was."

When she was eighteen, her stepfather, who was a line inspector, relocated the family to Canton, Illinois. Next door was a family, the Browns, with a thirteen-year-old daughter named Lil. "My God," Merle exclaimed, "when I seen her, I fell in love with her at first sight." Since Merle thought that Lil's older brother, Les, was a nice enough fellow, she started dating him "to be near her. So him and I, we went together. But the reason I went with him, really in my heart, was to get to be near her."

Merle and Les dated for several years. The Browns liked Merle, especially because she always seemed willing to have young Lil tag along on these dates. And Merle's parents could feel secure that Les wasn't taking liberties with their daughter, since his younger sister was with them. Merle and Les took in movies, went on picnics, and drove through the countryside—and young Lil accompanied them.

After a few years, Les relocated to Rock Falls for employment. Merle concocted a plan for her and Lil to go too. The two young women lived together, and Merle continued—at least for a while—to go out with Les.

From the beginning, Merle sensed that Lil "wasn't like me. I knew her feelings didn't run that way." But, she said, "I was just nice to her and she gradually learned to care for me." Eventually, Merle confessed her love, and, to her delight, Lil agreed to be with her. Merle and Lil stayed together for more than five decades. "We was never apart" is how Merle described it.

They were two small-town working-class women on their own, through the Great Depression, a world war, and a postwar decade that made war on queers. It could not have been easy. But to hear Merle tell it, their time together had more than its fair share of rewards.

First, they moved to Sterling, Illinois, where each found a job waitressing at a café. "We got our own place and boy, we did alright. We always made a living." When they wanted a night out, plenty of male customers were ready to escort them. "We never paid our way," Merle said. "Anywhere we wanted to go, we'd always get a date. We saved our money."

Every few years they'd relocate. "We've been everywhere," Merle recalled proudly. Once, they even got jobs on a ship. In 1952, after more than twenty-five years together, they settled in Chicago. For a long stretch, they worked in the establishment of a restaurant owner named Maury Saperstein. Lil was head waitress, and Merle often worked the night shift.

By today's standards, Chicago in the 1950s was not a great place to be a woman-loving woman. It was the McCarthy era, and along with the fierce anticommunist witch hunts came a "lavender scare." The *Tribune* frequently featured articles about the threat posed by perverts and moral degenerates. The police raided bars at will. Yes, there was a gay and lesbian community life, but it wasn't easy to find, and women had many fewer options than men. Even so, the possibility of building a network of lesbian friends was a lot greater in Chicago than in Sterling or Rock Falls.

But Merle, in her own words, "wasn't even interested." Though she claimed not to care what society thought ("I was headstrong"), she worried lest anyone find out about the two of them: "I knew, for my sake and for her sake, we had to go along. As long as we was working and making a living in the straight world, then we had to be straight. When we came home and were together, that was our business. But we conducted ourselves like ladies when we was out." Lots of people believed they were sisters, "so nobody thought anything about it." As far as Merle was concerned, "we had each other. We didn't need nobody."

From a contemporary perspective, Merle might be said to have lived her life deep in the closet. But Merle would have stared at you like you were nuts if you accused her of that. To this tough-skinned woman, she was merely being prudent. Lil was everything to her, and as long as she had Lil, why self-disclose?

As long as she had Lil: Soon after turning seventy, Lil became sick. It was terminal, and Merle nursed her at home through the final weeks of life. Merle had loved Lil for fifty-eight years, and now, in 1978, she faced life alone. In Merle's words, "I didn't care if I died or if I lived. I didn't care for nothing. I wished God had taken me right with her . . . I couldn't go to my straight friends and tell them. They didn't know how I felt. I had to keep that all inside of me."

Reading this part of the interview made me teary-eyed. What, I wondered, will this woman, who had never confided in anyone, do?

Luckily, this was 1978, not 1958 or 1938. In the 1970s, a new world was taking shape in Chicago. As some of the later essays in this book will reveal, a cohort of activist feminist lesbians was building community—a public community—like there was no tomorrow. Besides the bars, there were coffeehouses and restaurants, newspapers and softball teams, bookstores and community centers, and music concerts.

Merle went looking—through the telephone directory. "All I could find in there was gay bars," she remembered. "I'd call up and there'd be a man answering the phone, and I'd say to him 'any lesbians in there? I'd like to talk to them.'" Some bartenders just hung up, thinking it a crank call, but others engaged this strange old woman in conversation.

Finally, after months of this, she came across mention of a counseling service for lesbians. "My God, I thought I had hit the jackpot." Whenever she called, she'd get an answering machine, but "I would call, just to hear that voice, because I knew it was a lesbian talking, just to hear her voice on the recording."

One day, someone called back. She and Merle talked for hours, and soon other volunteers were calling her too. They enticed her out, to a service of the Metropolitan Community Church's Good Shepherd Parish and the social hour afterward. She asked her escort, Pat, "Are these all gay people?" Merle couldn't believe it. "I couldn't imagine it was that many. I thought to myself, 'My goodness, can't be. Now figure that!'" Soon she was going to lesbian bars, like His and Hers.

By the time Merle was interviewed in 1981, she had made a new life. Some of her younger friends were into the lesbian music scene and began taking her to concerts and music festivals. The first time she went to the Michigan Womyn's Music Festival, she was beside herself. "My God, there were ten thousand of them, just a whole ten thousand lesbians. Just think of that. A year ago, I'd give anything in the world if I could have just met one, and here they are, by the ten thousand."

It turned out that Merle had a bit of musical talent. Listening to women perform at bars and coffeehouses, she spontaneously improvised her own lyrics. The younger women, Merle chuckled, "get a bang out of a woman my age getting up and singing." At the Michigan festival, she was invited onto the stage. As she sang,

> Oh, I'd like to meet someone my age
> So come on, baby, and give me a call

women crowded the stage, eager to hug and kiss this woman more than twice their age.

Merle's story was unique to me, a real mind-bender. I say this not because there was no other life like hers, but because not many stories like this one have come down to us. Who knows how many working-class women, in small towns across America, made a life with another woman? They did it without big announcements, without family dramas, and without taking on labels—or even knowing of labels—that would have marked them as evil or sick.

And then there's the magic of Merle's rebirth. It's almost as if she was Rip Van Winkle, who sleeps for a generation and wakes up to discover a new world. Merle took hold of it with gusto, and the way she remade herself is inspirational.

2

The Struggle for Self-Acceptance: The Life of George Buse

Generations are vitally important in the study of history, as they often provide a sense of coherence to the experience of a group and an era. Think, for instance, of the way that the terms "baby boomers" and "millennials" are used to characterize a large cast of historical actors. This sense of generational difference is especially true in the case of LGBTQ history, where notions of identity, the development of community, and the capacity for collective activist resistance changed so dramatically across the twentieth century. Merle's story, told in the previous essay, provides one example of life for a particular generation. Born in 1902 in small-town America, she had no words to describe her feelings, no sense of any others who were like her, and no way of imagining being open about the love that she and Lil shared. Even as the world around her was changing, she remained in the box that defined the lives of most members of her generation. Only with the traumatic death of her life partner did she experience the impulse to peer outside, and she then discovered some of the dramatic ways that society was remaking itself.

The story of George Buse provides insight into the elements of continuity as well as change that someone born a bit more than two decades after Merle confronted. Buse donated a substantial collection of his personal papers to Gerber/Hart. Among the materials are transcripts of two oral histories conducted in the second half of

The interviews can be found in the George S. Buse Papers, Gerber/Hart Library and Archives.

the 1990s. Both are rich with details of Buse's life and his interior emotional struggles.

When Buse was interviewed, he was in his early seventies and a well-known figure in Chicago's LGBTQ community. Since the late 1970s, he had been a reporter for the LGBTQ press in the city. He had covered all three of the national Marches on Washington—in 1979, 1987, and 1993—and participated in many of the major local demonstrations, such as those in response to a wave of bar raids in 1979. In the early 1990s, he was among the first group of inductees into the Chicago LGBT Hall of Fame, an initiative of Mayor Richard M. Daley that was designed to honor members of the queer community. Yet, although he was very much engaged in the out-of-the-closet lifestyle of post-Stonewall activists, Buse himself, in narrating his life story, freely acknowledged what a long and painful struggle he put himself through before he was able to admit his gayness, come out of the closet, and commit himself to a life of activism.

* * *

Buse was born in Dubuque, Iowa, in 1924, the son of a pharmacist. Though a town of forty thousand, Dubuque as Buse remembered it was very much a part of the surrounding rural world of farms. Growing up in this environment in the 1930s, he recalled those years as "a very chaste period . . . sex wasn't on our minds all that much," and homosexuality was "never discussed, never . . . you'd hear occasional dirty jokes about it, maybe." By the time he was in high school, Buse "knew that [he] was different" and recognized "a very compelling need" to keep his feelings of difference secret.

In 1942, almost immediately after high school, Buse joined the marine corps. For him, World War II seemed to change everything—or almost everything. "Young men were out screwing around, going to the whore houses . . . talking about their sexual conquests . . . and that's when queer became apparent in my mind." He remembered his fellow marines talking about going out to "roll a few queers tonite . . . and beat the hell out of 'em." In this potentially dangerous environment, Buse "fell madly in love" with Ralph, another marine. They never had sex—it seemed far too risky—but in Buse's recollection "[they] were inseparable" and they developed "[their] own little secret language" that fostered their intimacy. Sadly, the two were assigned to different combat zones and never saw each other again.

After the war, Buse returned to the Midwest and used his GI benefits to go to college and graduate school, where he received a degree in journalism. He worked for a while as a stringer for Dubuque's daily newspaper, but the horrors of the war still weighed heavily on him. Those years were "the low point of my life," he told his interviewer. "Death is a daily reality . . . every day somebody you care about and loved, goddammit, has just been shot to pieces." The struggle led him to come to Chicago to attend seminary. It was a means to redeem himself after the brutal violence of the war. While in seminary, he did community service with youth in one of the city's settlement houses and became an admired mentor to many of the neighborhood's teenage boys. He saw in this evidence of the homosexual desires that he was still suppressing. "I would never touch one of those kids," he remembered, "yet there were deep feelings inside . . . I loved those boys."

Through all this, the suffering he had witnessed during World War II continued to affect him, and when he graduated from seminary, he decided to reenlist in the service, this time in the navy. Assigned to Japan, he served as a chaplain for several years, hoping to provide comfort and security to service members. Then he fell in love with his assistant, with whom he pursued his first sexually intimate relationship, until the navy discovered it. After going through "the psychological torment" of a naval intelligence interrogation, Buse was expelled from the service and, in 1964, at the age of forty, returned to Chicago, burdened by the disgrace of a dishonorable discharge. Initially unwilling to accept him into the ministry, the Presbyterian Church sent him to a psychiatrist who provided support for his reentry into the ministry. But, as a single man well into middle age, he was not an ideal choice to lead a congregation. He could only secure a part-time position with a very small congregation in the Rogers Park neighborhood, and, to supplement his income, he found employment as a medical social worker.

Buse spent more than a decade, from the mid-1960s to the late 1970s, trying to find a place for himself that brought both professional and personal satisfaction. His social work clients were primarily elderly individuals with serious health challenges and few economic resources. Eventually, this immersion in "the living tragedy of old people" was too much for him, and he quit the job.

Through these years, Buse had begun to participate in the social world of gay bars. He even attended an occasional meeting or event sponsored by Mattachine Midwest, Chicago's main gay activist organization in the late 1960s. But it extracted an emotional toll to keep this social world and personal identity separate from his public work life. As the 1970s wore on and an activist gay and lesbian world grew increasingly visible around him, he became deeply dissatisfied with his work in the church. He knew he was "not gonna come out of the closet to this congregation." Finally, he "couldn't stand the hypocrisy anymore," and he left the church entirely.

One of the changes that the gay liberation era of the 1970s brought was the creation of an LGBTQ press. In Chicago, the main paper in the late 1970s was *Gay Life*. With his education and some earlier experience in journalism, Buse walked into the office of *Gay Life* one day and told the publisher that he "wanted [to be] completely out of the closet . . . and I wanna do it by making myself useful." He was hired on the spot. "The pay was piss poor . . . the main thing was to be involved in journalism in the gay community." One of his first assignments was to cover the 1979 March on Washington for gay and lesbian rights. Held ten years after the Stonewall Uprising, it was the first such national protest of the movement. The march dramatically displayed for him the new world of out-of-the-closet queer life and activism that was taking shape across the United States. Buse continued this journalistic work into the 1990s, covering local stories as well as the national marches that took place in 1987 and 1993. The work as a journalist changed his life forever. "I've been an activist in the gay community since 1979," he proclaimed in his interview, and it led over time to his having "a hell of a good friendship network."

While Buse seemed to have fully adapted to the dramatic changes wrought by post-Stonewall activism, he remained acutely aware of how exceptional this was for a member of his generation. Most of his contemporaries were still "in hiding ... [They] never identified with the community ... They're still in the closet ... They're afraid ... they have nothing to fear, but they don't know that yet."

This generational ethic extracted its price on Buse, even as he personally had left it behind. "I don't have very many friends any-more of my age," he told his interviewer. The vast majority of his close relationships were among gay men who were more than a gen-eration younger than he was. With his health declining and physi-cal mobility becoming ever more challenging, he depended on their assistance. As he put it, "a typical day in my life is dictated not by my sexual orientation but by my physical degeneration." His gay-ness had brought discharge from the military after years of service. It kept him on the margins of the ministry in part-time positions. It brought him to embrace the liberation that gay journalism seemed to provide even as it meant he spent more than a decade earning barely subsistence wages. All this resulted in rather minimal social security benefits and no pension during his late sixties and early seventies.

The man who had abandoned the fear and caution of his gen-eration now was on the forefront of experiencing directly a newly emerging queer issue. Buse was discovering firsthand how "vitally important" it was for queer elders to "create our own families out of our own kind of people." As the century ended and a new one began, LGBTQ activists and organizations in Chicago and elsewhere would come to recognize the needs of elders as a critical issue facing the community.

3

Renee Hanover:
Always a Radical

Yes, generations are important, in the sense that they can provide
an organizing framework for understanding the broad cultural, social, and political environment of an era. But this framework should
not lead to the expectation of "we're all the same" life experiences.
The impact of region, race, gender, class, and so much more can
lead to highly individualized biographies. When placed alongside
the story of George Buse, the life of Renee Hanover, as it emerges
from two oral histories conducted in 1995, displays elements of both
commonality and difference.

The child of immigrants, Hanover was born in New York City in
1926, just two years after Buse. She grew up in poverty—"we were
starving during the Depression," she told her interviewer—and lived
in an environment in which left-wing militant protest was commonplace. At some point she joined the Communist Party, and, in 1951,
at the height of the McCarthy-era Red Scare, the party had her relocate to Chicago. Hanover also married and had children. She does
not reveal in the interview whether her husband was a Communist
Party member or at what point she left the party. But her experience
on the left made her, she proclaimed, "a radical way before" the protest era of the 1960s and the rise of a gay liberation movement.

At some point, Hanover and her husband separated, and, deciding she wanted to be a lawyer, she worked her way through col-

The interview can be found in the Jack Rinella Papers, Gerber/Hart Library and Archives.

lege and into law school while raising her three children. During these years, she also began to act on her attraction to women. A few months before graduation, in 1963–64, it somehow surfaced that she was a lesbian. The results were tragic. "I got thrown out of law school because I was gay, and my lover killed herself," she said. Eventually, Pearl Hart, one of her teachers and a well-known activist lawyer in Chicago, fought to get Hanover readmitted to the John Marshall School of Law, and she ultimately received her degree and was admitted to the bar.

From the start, Hanover brought an activist impulse to the study and practice of law. In the early 1960s, she helped put together a lawsuit to challenge the racial segregation of Chicago's lakefront beaches. She represented the Blackstone Rangers, a black youth gang that grew increasingly politicized in the 1960s and that was targeted by Chicago's police. She was an early participant in the Alliance to End Repression, a coalition of progressive organizations that formed in the city at the end of the 1960s. And she joined the National Lawyers Guild as well, which brought left-wing progressive lawyers together from around the country and strategized how legal cases could move struggles for justice and equality forward in the United States. Eventually Hanover served on its national executive board.

Even as she plunged into a left-wing legal activism associated with the radical movements of the 1960s, Hanover carried with her a determination to somehow change the way that gays and lesbians were treated by society. After her lover's suicide, she told her interviewer, "it was then that I said . . . 'Nobody is going to kill themselves over this anymore.'" Toward the end of the 1960s, she made a connection with the Mattachine Society, at that point the main LGBTQ organization in Chicago and hardly representative of the kind of militant radical politics that appealed to Hanover. But, in 1969, the same year as the Stonewall Uprising, David Stienecker, a Mattachine member, published a photo of a cop in Chicago, Officer Manley, who dressed in street clothes, entrapped large numbers of gay men, and then arrested them on sex charges. Manley came to Stienecker's home and arrested him for defamation of character. Hanover took the case and succeeded in getting the charges dismissed.

By this time, the gay liberation impulse had hit Chicago, and Hanover threw herself into it. She attended the first meetings in Hyde Park that led to the founding of Chicago Gay Liberation. "We were building up the left part of the movement," Hanover told her interviewer. "The really 'stick it in your face' movement." At some point, a group of lesbians split off and began meeting separately at the apartment of Vernita Grey, who would become a key Chicago activist over the next decades. For Hanover, it was unbelievably exciting. "It was the first time any of us had been in a room with wall-to-wall lesbians," she recalled. "It just blew our minds, just absolutely blew our minds . . . You would have seen twenty women grinning for three hours straight."

Hanover quickly found herself taking on an array of LGBTQ-related legal cases. Early in 1970, when Chicago Gay Liberation decided to hold a public dance at the city's Coliseum, Hanover acted as negotiator with the police to make sure that no arrests occurred. A couple of thousand people came to the dance, and it was a historic moment in Chicago's history, since up until that point, as Hanover explained, "you weren't allowed dancing in gay bars." Soon, students at campuses across the Chicago region were planning dances of their own, and Hanover kept arranging meetings with local police to ward off interventions. When several young Mexicans were arrested by police for violating the city's cross-dressing law—they were all wearing dresses—Hanover defended them in court and persuaded the judge to dismiss the charges. As more previously married women came out as lesbians and faced court suits from their ex-husbands who challenged their right to custody of their children, Hanover came to their defense as well. Nor did she hesitate to aim her legal skills at injustices within the community. It was quite common in the 1960s and 1970s for gay and lesbian bars to insist on multiple pieces of identity from African Americans as a way of keeping them out. When several black lesbians told her about their experience with a North Side bar, Hanover threatened to file race discrimination charges against the owner. The bar changed its practices.

Of all the legal initiatives that Hanover described, one that especially stood out for me was her handling of police entrapment in public restrooms. At a time when the vast majority of gay men were in the closet and when there were few spaces for gay and bisexual men to meet, public restrooms were a common site where men searched for sex. Officer Manley was only the most outrageous example of plainclothes officers enticing such men to make sexual advances and then arresting them on morals charges. Across the city, these were likely happening on a daily basis. For closeted men, such arrests at the very least meant public shaming. But it could also mean the loss of a job and an arrest and conviction record that would follow them for the rest of their lives. Arrestees often hastily pled guilty as a way of avoiding a public trial.

Hanover made these police practices a primary target of her legal activism. Over time, she said, she accumulated "sketches of every men's room in this town, public men's rooms . . . because when I had the cases, I had to say, 'Well, how could you see them from here.'" She persuaded clients to ask for a jury trial, knowing that the weakness of the police testimony under cross-examination would either get the charges dismissed or result in a jury's acquittal. Her description of a common courtroom experience captures the fear that enveloped so many gay and bisexual men's lives in the 1960s and 1970s. "I would sit with gay guys in court when they would be arrested in these bathrooms," she remembered. "They would be shaking like mad. Just shaking. Afraid they would lose their jobs. Afraid that they would lose . . . everything else. I would sit there and hold their hands and just say to them . . . 'These are just man-made laws. We are going to change these laws. This has nothing to do with the dignity of us as individuals.'"

In reflecting on her career, Hanover described herself as "the first lesbian attorney out in the country." While I cannot confirm with certainty that this is true, it may very well be. Lambda Legal Defense

and Education Fund, which became the leading LGBTQ legal organization in the US, was not founded until 1973. Other organizations,
like the National Center for Lesbian Rights and the ACLU's Gay and
Lesbian Rights Project, came even later. But whether or not she was
the first, Hanover was definitely a pioneer, ahead of her generation
in her outspoken defense of LGBTQ people. "It is very hard to tell
someone how awful it was in that period," she recalled. Grounded
in a lifetime of activism and values that she absorbed on the left,
Hanover displayed extraordinary courage and an unwavering commitment to let no injustice go unchallenged. Her work is even more
impressive when one realizes that she took many of these cases pro
bono, since her clients were often not in a position to pay legal fees.
While many factors help explain the growing visibility of LGBTQ
people in Chicago and across the United States in the last decades
of the twentieth century, the fierce determination of an individual
like Renee Hanover was certainly a key element in the changes that
have come since the 1960s.

4

Max Smith: A Gay Liberationist at Heart

For Merle, for Buse, and for Hanover, coming out was a challenge. They were raised during decades when the notion of being openly gay or lesbian, of declaring one's sexual identity to others, was barely imaginable. They faced a profound cultural silence about their sexuality, a silence that tended to be broken only when the voice of oppression made itself heard.

The baby boom generation was the first for whom, among some at least, coming out came to be seen as normative. Born in the years after World War II, many baby boomers were teenagers or young adults during the turbulent years of the 1960s, when protest was erupting across the United States and challenging authority seemed the thing to do. The Stonewall Uprising of 1969 was very much a product of baby boomers. Young gay men and transwomen, many of them people of color, said no in the most dramatic way possible to police harassment.

The story of Max Smith very much captures this newly emerging ethic. Born in Hickory, North Carolina, in 1954, the year of the historic *Brown v. Board of Education* Supreme Court decision that declared legally sanctioned racial segregation of schools unconstitutional, Smith nonetheless spent his childhood in a South in which "there was absolute, state-mandated apartheid." "I went to an all-black school," he recalled, "lived in an all-black neighborhood,

The interview can be found in the Jack Rinella Papers, Gerber/Hart Library and Archives.

knew two non-black people before I was twelve years old." Labeled "a sissy" as a young boy, he determined to get involved in sports, to learn "to walk in the proper way," and to present himself as "masculine." Dating girls in junior high and in high school, he succeeded in avoiding any suspicions of being queer.

Smith escaped the South in 1972 to attend Michigan State University in East Lansing. Stonewall and the birth of gay liberation had happened only three years earlier, but campuses were among the places where the liberation impulse most quickly found a welcoming home. Michigan State already had a student group called the Gay Liberation Council when Smith arrived. He threw himself into it. "We were gay liberationists at heart. We marched in the Detroit Gay Day Freedom Parade," he recalled. "We were in the vanguard." His fellow students were impressed enough that they elected him president of the group. Reflecting on those years, Smith proudly asserted that "we vowed, those of us who were in the group, to always be out of the closet in our future jobs after graduation into the real world."

Deciding to settle in Chicago after getting his degree, he immediately sought out the city's queer community. In college he had read *The Lord Is My Shepherd and Knows That I Am Gay*, a memoir by the Reverend Troy Perry, who had founded the LGBTQ-welcoming Metropolitan Community Church. "The very first week that I moved to Chicago I attended the Good Shepherd Parish MCC," he told his interviewer. It "gave me a tremendous amount of self-understanding and I was very anxious to attend a church that would be accepting of my sexuality." Smith found the environment friendly and was pleased with the congregation's overt commitment to racial justice. He attended services every Sunday and soon was elected to its board of directors.

Still in his early twenties, Smith threw himself into the world of queer activism that was growing rapidly and becoming more visible in Chicago in the second half of the 1970s. He joined the Illinois Lesbian and Gay Rights Task Force, which lobbied the city council and the state legislature for antidiscrimination legislation. When the

Gay and Lesbian Coalition of Metropolitan Chicago formed, Smith was part of that as well. As he described it, "gay bars from all over town, gay political, religious, social, athletic, all the different types of gay groups that you can think of, came together." When police raids or legislative hearings required mobilizing people for demonstrations, Smith used the phone tree of contacts he had developed as a tool for reaching people quickly. He especially remembered Anita Bryant's visit to Chicago in June 1977, a week after her campaign to repeal antidiscrimination legislation in Dade County, Florida, had succeeded. "As soon as I came up from the subway station, it was this huge crowd and I joined right in," he recounted enthusiastically. There was "an energy that just grew and grew. At that time, the spirit of the lesbian/gay community was very young and very vibrant and an event like that could really make it expand rapidly . . . It made people feel good and encouraged people to more activism." Chicagoans who were there remember it as a pivotal event that mobilized the community as nothing had before. Two weeks later, Chicago's Pride March was noticeably larger than it had ever been.

Smith continued to pursue his activist path. Early in 1979, he learned that, on the same weekend as the March on Washington that was scheduled for October, there would be the "first-ever" Third World Lesbian and Gay Conference. If he had any hesitation about traveling to Washington for the march, this announcement settled it. Smith remembered that weekend vividly: "I think for the first time, there was a real, real consciousness on the part of thousands and thousands of people that they were very much in this together, nationwide." And the Third World Conference stimulated that same sense of an expansive togetherness. "I met black lesbian and gay people from all over the country," he recalled. Meeting on the historically black Howard University campus, this gathering of activists formed the National Coalition of Black Lesbians and Gays. "It was the first national black lesbian and gay organization," and Smith was part of its creation.

Since his arrival in Chicago, Smith had been working for the *Chicago Tribune* selling real estate advertising. The *Tribune* was a politically conservative paper. In the 1950s it had aggressively propagated the claims that the federal government was filled with sexual perverts who were a danger to the nation. Even through the 1970s, it was still publishing stories about the police raids of gay bars without ever condemning the actions. Although Smith was an activist in the community, he had kept his identity private on the job. He did have a small number of comrades at the *Tribune* whom he had met at various community events, but in the workplace they remained discreet about their gayness. There were no protections against discrimination in Chicago, and so the world of work and the world of community activism for most LGBTQ people still remained quite separate and distinct.

Then, in 1979, in the wake of the March on Washington and the formation of a national network of African American gays and lesbians, Smith was invited to appear on a local television talk show. As he recalled it, executives at the *Tribune* were "not particularly tickled over an employee appearing on such a television show." Despite strong performance evaluations, "a firing occurred of yours truly on the grounds of sexual orientation." But, activist that he was, the dismissal did not stop Smith. In fact, he transformed it into an opportunity for more visible activism. "I presented my information at the Chicago City Council in the hearing . . . for the passage of the City Human Rights Ordinance." Smith's evidence of discrimination proved "really instrumental in convincing the Council to pass it out of Committee and to take a floor vote." While the council as a whole was not yet ready to support such a law, the drama of his testimony and the hearings brought unprecedented local media attention to discrimination in the workforce. More and more opportunities came his way to be on radio talk shows. After one dialogue on an AM radio show, the producers told Smith that "they got more telephone calls to their station the night a gay rights dialogue was their topic than they had gotten in weeks."

Smith survived his firing by the *Tribune* and went on to have a successful career in retail sales. But the situation he faced serves as a reminder that the 1970s were very much a transitional decade. On one hand, some young adults were creating a whole new world of visible, militant, activist community. But oppression was still alive and well, and most LGBTQ people—whether of older generations or even among many baby boomers—were holding on to the protections of staying in the closet. It would take the tragedy of the AIDS epidemic in the 1980s and 1990s for that to change forever.

5

The Gay Liberation Era in Chicago

The year 2019 marked the fiftieth anniversary of the Stonewall Uprising in New York and the birth of what was described at the time as the "gay liberation" movement. Across the United States and, indeed, around the world, a massive number of events commemorated this decisive moment in LGBTQ history. As the life stories of Renee Hanover and Max Smith have demonstrated, already by the early 1970s this liberation impulse had spread to Chicago and the Midwest.

Valuable and compelling as the oral histories of individuals are for making history come alive, these recollections alone are insufficient to flesh out the past. We need historical records—archives—in order to reconstruct history in all its complexities. Documents that describe the work of an activist organization, the planning of a major event or campaign, or the social and cultural life of a community are the essential raw materials of history.

From the start, LGBTQ organizations produced periodicals of one sort or another—newsletters, magazines, journals, newspapers—that recorded the work of activists and the internal dynamics of the group. Most of these did not have massive circulation or long runs. Yet they do often provide thorough and detailed reports on local events and the work of the organization. They also frequently con-

The newsletters of Chicago Gay Liberation and Chicago Gay Activists can be found in the periodicals collection at Gerber/Hart Library and Archives.

tain opinion pieces and commentary written by local activists that give a vivid sense of the times.

Two such periodicals are the newsletters produced by Chicago Gay Liberation and the Chicago Gay Alliance. These were two of the very earliest post-Stonewall organizations to form in Chicago. The newsletters at Gerber/Hart stretch from 1970 to 1972, and they report on the broad range of activities that the groups engaged in, the demonstrations they organized, and the tensions and challenges they each confronted.

At first glance, the story that unfolds in Chicago seems to parallel what has become the standard narrative that historians have constructed of early post-Stonewall activism in New York. In the wake of Stonewall, a group calling itself the Gay Liberation Front quickly formed in New York. Self-declared militant revolutionaries, they conducted sassy public actions, urged people to come out, declared solidarity with other radical movements of the day, and displayed that solidarity by participating as openly queer contingents in marches against the Vietnam War and at rallies in support of the Black Panther Party. Within months, a group of white gay men split from the GLF and formed the Gay Activists Alliance. It, too, was committed to militant public action, but it broke with the multi-issue coalition politics of the Gay Liberation Front and declared itself solely focused on gay issues.

Reading the *Chicago Gay Liberation Newsletter*, one immediately encounters its militancy and its multi-issue orientation. Besides organizing a Pride March and Rally in June 1970—Chicago was one of only three cities that did this—and conducting demonstrations at restaurants that refused to serve gay customers, it also sent a contingent to participate in the march commemorating those who died in the atomic bombing of Hiroshima. It organized support for the Venceremos Brigade, a group of young radicals who were backing the Cuban revolution and defying the US boycott of the island nation. One of its newsletters contained a report on the Revolutionary People's Party Convention, held in Philadelphia in September 1970 and organized by the Black Panther Party. Chicago Gay Liberation included both a women's caucus and a black caucus, which worked to keep issues of sexism and racism in the vision of the organization while also remaining active in the organization as a whole.

The October 1970 issue of the newsletter reported that Chicago Gay Liberation was experiencing a "schism." A large group of white gay men decided to secede from the organization because it was "too political, too radical" and was "allying itself too closely to Movement groups." They formed a new group, the Chicago Gay Alliance. The first issue of the CGA newsletter, published in November 1970, announced that "our politics are that of homosexuality." Another article declared that "the most important part of liberation is personal." CGA definitely remained a militant organization. It planned and conducted public demonstrations that could be rowdy and disruptive. But it continued to proclaim that CGA "is devoted *solely* [emphasis in original] to the politics of homosexuality."

Although this seems to mirror what had happened a few months earlier in New York, a closer reading of the newsletters leads to a more complicated and nuanced analysis. Chicago Gay Liberation, for instance, might declare itself a revolutionary organization, but a surprisingly large number of its demonstrations were focused on obtaining the right to dance. The famous retort attributed to anarchist Emma Goldman notwithstanding ("If I can't dance, it's not my revolution"), one could reasonably argue that the right to dance was not the cutting edge of revolutionary change in American society. Meanwhile, though CGA stated that its only focus was on homosexuality, its newsletter reported on gay contingents at antiwar marches, provided its readers with information about the Hiroshima Day rally, and joined in a broad coalition action to protest President Richard Nixon's appearance in Chicago. At least in Chicago, the divide between revolutionary and reformist, between multi-issue and single-issue politics, was a good deal hazier than it might seem upon first analysis.

Perhaps what the newsletters most dramatically capture was the intensity and extent of activism in this three-year period. Especially when one considers that both organizations were run entirely on volunteer labor and had almost no budget to speak of, the amount of work they did in this three-year period was huge. Between them, they organized protests against police harassment and violence. Although bar raids and arrests occurred throughout the United States, Chicago had an especially bad record. CGA's newsletter of December 1971 declared that "Chicago still remains the most oppressive major city in the U.S. . . . The reason is the outrageous harassment from Mayor Daley and his police." Activists also demonstrated against gay bars that discriminated to keep women and people of color out and against other commercial establishments that discriminated against LGBTQ people. They appeared on radio and TV shows at a time when a visible queer presence was still extremely rare. They maintained a speakers' bureau and sent speakers to a number of high schools in the greater Chicago area. They polled candidates for Chicago's city council, and they testified at city council hearings about the need to enact laws banning discrimination. They helped organize student groups on campuses around the state. CGA opened Chicago's first community center for LGBTQ people, located in a house at 171 Elm Street in the Old Town neighborhood. CGA maintained a mailing list of 1,300, at a time when doing a hard-copy mailing was the main way to communicate to people en masse, and that involved a lot of work. CGA likewise produced three thousand copies of its newsletter and distributed it in many venues across the city. By January 1971, the work of Chicago Gay Liberation, the Chicago Gay Alliance, and other post-Stonewall groups had mobilized widely enough that a citywide gathering of activists attracted several hundred people. Just two years earlier, such a large turnout would have been unimaginable.

Today, when so many LGBTQ organizations have paid staff, when many elected officials seek out LGBTQ endorsements, and when there is so much cultural visibility and attention from news media, it can be hard to appreciate just how cutting edge the work of these two early post-Stonewall organizations in Chicago was. It made a big difference. It created a foundation upon which later organizations and activists built. The newsletters of these two organizations offer vivid documentation of the activism that exploded in these years.

As a concluding note, let me add that the process of research into one topic often piques one's curiosity about others. That was certainly the case as I read these two organizational newsletters. As someone who taught at the University of Illinois at Chicago for fifteen years, I was struck by how frequently it turned up in these newsletters. As early as May 1970, the campus was hosting "gay" dances. In June, during what was the first "Pride Week" in Chicago, it hosted four days of workshops on LGBTQ topics and issues. And, for a stretch of time, the Sunday night meetings of Chicago Gay Liberation were held on the campus at Halsted and Harrison Streets. Moreover, these newsletters make clear that UIC was not the only campus where gay liberation activities were taking place. Student groups were proliferating in the Chicago area and across the state—at the University of Chicago and at Northwestern University; at Roosevelt University; and at Northern Illinois University, Illinois State University, and the University of Illinois in Champaign-Urbana.

Clearly, the culture and environment of universities at the end of the 1960s were hospitable to and perhaps even encouraging of this new gay liberation impulse. As we saw in the story of Max Smith, these groups served as training grounds for activists who would continue their movement work through the 1970s and beyond. Reconstructing the histories of campus activism will provide a fuller picture of the early gay liberation era.

6

A Queer Radical's Story: Step May and Chicago Gay Liberation

While the newsletters of Chicago Gay Liberation and the Chicago Gay Alliance provide a sense of the activism taking shape in Chicago in the immediate post-Stonewall years, the experience of individuals remains shadowy. Who were these first post-Stonewall activists? How did they make their way into this new and more militant movement? In what ways were these times hospitable for transforming individuals into queer activists? Seeing through the eyes of an individual can make the broad contours of this growing movement and its impact on real lives more concrete.

Step May was one such individual. The son of Jewish refugees who had fled Nazi Germany, May grew up in rural America, on a poultry farm near Lake Ontario in upstate New York. At the age of thirteen, he came upon the word "homosexual" and knew that it described him. Considered to be "fruity and a fairy" by many of his peers, he found a group of friends that accepted him and helped him make it through high school. Winning admission to the University of Chicago, he moved to the campus on Chicago's South Side in the fall of 1965.

May's family was not political at all, and certainly not leftists. But by the time he arrived at the University of Chicago, protest against the escalating war in Vietnam was growing fast. May remained detached from it at first, but in his sophomore year, when the federal

The interview can be found in the Jack Rinella Papers, Gerber/Hart Library and Archives.

government proposed ending automatic draft deferments for college students, he became involved in Students against the Rank. Many of its members were also part of SDS—Students for a Democratic Society—the key New Left activist campus group in the 1960s. "I did not know what SDS was all about," May recalled, and "I had absolutely no idea of what 'the left' was." But soon he found himself occupying a campus building, an act that led to his suspension from the college. In order to maintain his deferment for the draft, he signed up for VISTA, one of President Lyndon Johnson's Great Society programs, and he found himself in the South doing community service work and surrounded by radical activists in the black freedom movement of those years. Before long, May counted himself in the ranks of the left. When he returned to the University of Chicago in March 1969, he immediately joined SDS and threw himself not only into antiwar activities but also into support for black activism and the emerging women's liberation movement.

That spring, a couple of months before the Stonewall protests in New York and the founding of the Gay Liberation Front, May saw an ad in the *Maroon*, the campus student newspaper, that said "Gay Power" and had a box number for mailing a reply. May wrote a note and learned that there would be a meeting a few days later. He remembers about ten other students showing up, all tense and nervous. They listened to the student who called the meeting, David Goldman, talk about how student homophile leagues had formed on a few campuses and how he wanted to start one at the University of Chicago. "Here I was so political," May recalled, "and, even though he was speaking in political terms, it still didn't really connect with me . . . I never made the connection that what was happening to me as a gay person was also a form of oppression. I never used that word, oppression, to apply to a group of gay people."

May left Chicago again in the summer of 1969 to do antiwar organizing at a GI coffeehouse in Columbia, South Carolina. The place was filled with radical materials for GIs to read, and May remembered seeing an issue of the *Village Voice*, a politically progressive New York newspaper, that had an article about "this riot of gay people in Greenwich Village." Returning to school in the fall, he saw another ad in the *Maroon*. As he recalled it, the ad said, "Tired of Gay Oppression?" and had a phone number to call. "It took me a long time to get up the nerve to call," May told Gregory Sprague, the interviewer who recorded his story, but eventually he did and showed up at the second meeting. "That was when I really took off in the gay liberation movement," he recounted. "It all fell together for me ... I had a lot of energy ... I immediately kind of catapulted to the leadership at that very meeting." He met Henry Wiemhoff, who had placed the ad in the *Maroon*, and Murray Edelman and Libby Hamlan, who would both become active in gay liberation. By this time, May was thoroughly radicalized because of his VISTA work in the South and his antiwar organizing. As he put it, "one thing that was very kind of unique about my functioning in Chicago was that I was ... very open about gay liberation to the left and a very open revolutionary socialist in Gay Liberation."

In May's view, he provided "a lot of the militancy. I was always proposing militant actions ... let's get out on the street and yell. Let's demonstrate." In practice, a major focus of that early militancy was seizing public space for dancing as same-sex couples. May proposed going to one of the dances held in the campus residence halls. "We were all scared to death," he remembered, but the experience was so exhilarating that they decided to hold a dance of their own. The university recognized them as a group and gave them permission for the event, and soon these young gay liberationists were publicizing the dance in gay and lesbian bars on both the South and North Sides of the city. Hundreds showed up. "It was a wild success," May remembered. "We were all just delirious."

It may seem odd at this distance in time that a radical, self-declared "revolutionary socialist" would find himself ecstatic because he successfully helped carry off the planning for a dance. But, at the time, there was no public dancing by same-sex couples in bars or clubs in Chicago. Such behavior was grounds for arresting both the patrons and the employees of the bar. The fact that expressing one's sexual identity in a public setting through the act of dancing could be so thrilling captures the intensity of the oppression in this era.

By early spring, gay liberation groups were springing up on the North Side and on several of the other campuses in the Chicago area. In June 1970, Step May helped organize the first Pride March in Chicago to commemorate the Stonewall Uprising in New York the year before. The demonstrators marched from Bughouse Square to Grant Park. It was much smaller than the dances that had been held. Fewer than two hundred people showed up. But, as May described it, "it was very much a march . . . we were chanting and . . . holding hands. We had signs: 'Gay Liberation Now.'"

A few weeks after that first Pride March, May left Chicago again for a couple of months, this time as part of a Venceremos Brigade to Cuba. By the time he returned in October, Chicago Gay Liberation had fractured. A women's caucus had formed, with the goal of putting more attention on feminist issues and creating a separate space for discussions of sexism. A large number of the white men in the organization had left as well, rebelling at the insistence of people of color in the organization that Chicago Gay Liberation pay attention to issues of racial justice. As May put it, it was "the old fight between single issue and multi-issue." With his radical views, May naturally felt himself at odds with those who had split away to form the Chicago Gay Alliance. "They couldn't even stomach the word activist in the name of their organization," he told Sprague. May himself "strongly disagreed with the whole idea that gay liberation should be a single-issue movement . . . I felt that Gay Liberation had to formalize with other movements of the oppressed." With most of the women, the people of color, and the white gay men leaving Chicago Gay Liberation for other groups, CGL quickly faded from the scene. May became active for a while in a new group, the Chicago Gay People's Legal Committee, which Renee Hanover had set up and which was connected to the National Lawyers Guild. Finally, in 1974, he left Chicago and settled in Los Angeles, where he continued his gay liberation activism in a local radical group, the Lavender and Red Union.

Chicago Gay Liberation comprised only a brief moment in the history of LGBTQ activism in Chicago. But as May's reminiscences suggest, it was a critical moment, one that helped provoke the explosive growth of a new, more visible, and more militant activism in the Windy City.

7

The Transvestite Legal Committee

The last decade has seen the growth of an unprecedented level of attention to transgender issues and identity. Some of it is due to a heightened cultural visibility. The success of a television series like *Transparent*, the attention that Laverne Cox has received because of her role in *Orange Is the New Black*, and the celebrity status of someone like Caitlyn Jenner put transgender in the spotlight of popular culture. Some of the attention is the unfortunate result of oppression, particularly the violence directed at transwomen and the proliferation of state legislative attempts to restrict access to public restrooms. And some of the focus is the result of important steps forward politically, like the election to public office in 2017 of openly transgender political candidates. This attention functions as both cause and effect. It is an indicator of an intensified level of political organizing around transgender issues, and, at the same time, it contributes to the creation and spread of even more activism.

It would be a mistake, however, to let media recognition serve as a decisive historical marker of transgender activism. Young transpeople were a critical part of the Stonewall Uprising in 1969. Intentional efforts at building support networks and providing community education date back at least to the start of the 1970s. In New York, transgender activists like Marsha P. Johnson and Sylvia Rivera

The material on the Transvestite Legal Committee can be found in the William B. Kelley Papers, Gerber/Hart Library and Archives.

were highly visible, and they created a group called STAR—Street Transvestite Action Revolutionaries. Did Chicago have something comparable?

Bill Kelley was an activist with over half a century of involvement with the movement in Chicago. He was also something of a pack rat who, thankfully, saved every piece of movement-related material that came into his hands. Within his massive collection of papers is a folder that reveals that militant radical activism existed among transgender people in Chicago at the height of the gay liberation era.

The Transgender Legal Committee formed early in 1971, at a time when Chicago Gay Liberation had split into several of its component constituencies. A strong motivating force behind its creation was the brutal slaying in November 1970 of James Clay, an unarmed African American transwoman, who was shot in the back by Chicago police. No police officers were ever charged in the killing, and it remained a deep source of anger among activists, who organized protests in response, though without much effect. It also made clear the need to focus on the specific issues faced by transpeople, particularly transwomen of color.

The Transvestite Legal Committee provided support and information for its constituents. It put together a multipart document, "Legal Aspects of Transexualism and Information on Administrative Procedures," that offered guidance on how to get one's name changed on a birth certificate, a driver's license, and a social security card; how to deal with the military draft; and the implications of undergoing a gender change in terms of access to marriage. TLC also conducted a "Transvestites Law School" in which it held classes on the laws that impinged on transpeople, on how best to navigate the legal system if one were arrested, and on what it described as "street survival," since some of its constituents were homeless and also engaged in sex work. At a time when police raids of LGBTQ meeting places were commonplace, and when many gay bars engaged in discriminatory exclusionary policies toward transgender individuals and people of color, TLC organized social events for its constituency, such as dances and balls where well-known female impersonators performed. It also compiled a guide to safe spaces where local female impersonators performed and transvestites were welcome. Chicago sites included places on the North and South Sides, and in the Near North neighborhood not far from the city's downtown. Interestingly, the list also included the names of clubs in a broad swath of American cities stretching from coast to coast. Boston, Indianapolis, Detroit, Houston, Kansas City, Minneapolis, and Los Angeles are just some of the places named. This implies that something of a national network of communication within the trans population existed, as well as a geographic mobility.

But TLC was much more than an information service. Its newsletter offered ample evidence of a militant activism that pressed hard against the pervasive oppression that LGBTQ people generally— and transgender individuals especially—encountered in this era. Pushing against the isolation that many faced, it urged transvestites and transsexuals to come together as a "distinct ethnic community." Not surprisingly, TLC particularly targeted the police. At a time when mainstream media showed little empathy for the conditions of transgender life and rarely covered news about the community, its newsletter publicized events ranging from the arrest of individuals for cross-dressing to the murders of transwomen and the callous lack of concern that the criminal justice system displayed toward such violence. TLC sent a letter to the Chicago Police Department demanding an end to the harassment of transgender people on the streets and in bars and called for the creation of an LGBTQ advisory group with the power to monitor police behavior and hold them accountable. It also sent a letter to the Chicago District Attorney's office that charges be dropped against those arrested for cross-dressing. The fine for such a charge could be as high as $100, a significant amount of money at that time for individuals who often were living on the margins economically. TLC also addressed the needs of those in jail. It protested the way trans inmates were treated in the Cook County Jail. They received fewer privileges than other inmates—less recreational time outdoors in the yard and less access to television.

TLC also displayed a willingness to challenge mistreatment from within the LGBTQ community. When Douglas Middleton, the owner of Another Place, a popular bar on the South Side, tore down a poster that TLC had posted in the bar, TLC went on the offensive. It picketed the bar and distributed flyers that declared that Middleton needed to "protect and serve the black gay community." Employing some of the militant rhetoric of the era, the flyer said that "people like Douglas Middleton need to be smashed out of the fucking state!!!"

TLC frequently participated in the actions and projects of other LGBTQ groups in these early years of the post-Stonewall gay liberation movement. It reprinted and distributed the flyers of Chicago Gay Liberation with its militant, radical rhetoric. "We refuse to remain silent any longer," one of them declared. "The gay revolution is here to stay!" In February 1972, TLC attended a meeting in Chicago of the National Coalition of Gay Organizations in which activists drew up a platform to present to the Democratic Party at its national convention later in the year. The platform contained a wide-ranging list of demands, including the elimination of laws that banned the wearing of clothing of "the opposite sex." Later that year, TLC challenged the Illinois delegation to the national convention for not "even tokenly" representing transvestites and transsexuals.

The TLC documents only cover the years 1971 and 1972. I don't know how much longer it lasted, what happened to its members, or even who those members were. The most significant clue about who was most active in the organization and who its primary constituents were comes from the location of its meetings. Unlike almost all of the other emerging LGBTQ liberation groups at this time in Chicago, a high proportion of its meetings were held on the South Side, where the African American population was especially concentrated. A fuller history of the organization and its work can provide important glimpses into the state of transgender life and consciousness in an era before this constituency began capturing more public attention.

8

A National Network under the Radar: The Transvestite Information Service

The work done by Chicago Gay Liberation, the Chicago Gay Alliance, and the Transvestite Legal Committee can easily create the sense that this is what the early 1970s was like: an angry, open militancy erupting across the queer population. But the activists who were part of these organizations represented only a tiny segment of queer America. The overwhelming majority were still in the closet, still keeping their identity a secret. Many were living as cisgender heterosexuals. Others moved in an LGBTQ social world but kept that portion of their lives entirely apart from work, family, and straight friends.

The history of the Transvestite Information Service offers a glimpse into one segment of this population, a segment whose efforts to connect and break through an oppressive isolation were completely unknown to me. TVIS, as it often described itself, was established in 1971 in, of all places, Spencer, North Carolina, a community of barely three thousand people, halfway between Charlotte and Greensboro. Its founder was a man by the name of James Howell. Not much information about him appears in the TVIS newsletter or correspondence, other than that he was a biological male who was deeply attached to wearing female clothing. But he was obviously also an individual who cared intensely about building commu-

The material on the Transvestite Information Service can be found in the William B. Kelley Papers, Gerber/Hart Library and Archives.

nity among transvestites. He wanted to make life easier for a group of individuals for whom, at that time in history, there was little support and understanding and many of whom lived in relative isolation from others like themselves. Howell described the organization as "a nationwide non-profit public service for transvestites."

The documents about TVIS that I found in Bill Kelley's papers largely consist of newsletters that Howell produced between 1971 and 1973. One of the things that immediately becomes apparent is that, by the time Howell founded TVIS and started circulating his newsletter, he had already built a vast network among transvestites. Letters poured in from across the country. Participants in the network came from communities such as Marion, Indiana; Largo, Florida; Lansing, Illinois; Mountain View, California; Beachwood, Ohio; Hartford, Connecticut; Pontiac, Michigan; Phoenix, Arizona; and Ossining, New York. Clearly a web of connections must have existed before Howell formed his organization and began publishing and circulating his newsletter.

Besides cutting through the isolation that many of these gender-crossing individuals must have experienced, TVIS set out to provide advice to its subscribers. The December 1972 newsletter, for instance, included contact information for a list of "counselors." Some of it was organized by identity: bisexual, heterosexual, homosexual, and transsexual. Some of it was based on sexual practice. There was, for instance, a counselor for those who engaged in "Bondage/ Domination." There was a religious advisor, a home-and-family acceptance advisor, a counselor for wives, and a "public appearance improvement advisor" whose goal was to help individuals "improve your girl-self." Readers also turned to Howell for information about the legal issues that transvestites faced in different parts of the US. Howell apparently had done considerable research on state and local laws that criminalized wearing the clothing of what was then commonly referred to as "the opposite sex."

The life stories that emerge from these newsletters are compelling. Howell recognized that virtually every transvestite was con-

fronted by the issue of how open they should be about their identity. "Is It Wise to Be Honest with ALL Your Relatives?" he asked in
one of the newsletters, calling it "one of the greatest questions we
as transvestites have." Howell strove to make the newsletter a place
where readers could share experiences by having a "Speak Up and
Be Heard" section. Some readers submitted essays that were autobiographical. More often, the individual stories emerge in a letter
to the editor. In some cases, the letters provide a glimpse into the
intense pressures that many of the readers faced. As "Joe from New
Jersey" wrote in the November 1971 newsletter, "we are always living in fear. If we are found out, some of us will lose the love of a
family and all we will have left is shame and disgust." But there were
also letters that provided a counternarrative to the one of fear and
vulnerability. In that same newsletter, "Barbara from Connecticut"
posed the question, "Can a transvestite really be happy?" And her
unequivocal answer was "Yes."

Readers of the newsletter were not restricted to transvestites
themselves. Based on the letters that Howell chose to print, family members were also deeply engaged. There were letters, for instance, from the adult children of transvestites. Among the most
emotionally powerful were those that came from wives. The writers describe the relationship with their husband, how knowledge of
their husband's cross-dressing unfolded over time, and how their
marriage changed because of it. A wife from Baldwin, New York, informed readers that, contrary to what many might assume, the relationship proved "very rewarding and successful." She was not alone
in that evaluation. Another wife, who only identified herself as being from California, offered a touching account of her evolving marriage. She described how, over time, she moved from surprise and
discomfort to greater closeness and intimacy. One Christmas, when
her children were nine and eleven, she had them ask their father to
spend the whole day "as the girl he was." The result, she wrote, was
"the happiest I have ever seen him." It made the day "sparkle to see
the joy in his eyes and the love he had for us all." At a time when

there was little approval in the culture for transgender lives and experience, one can only imagine the satisfaction that it brought many subscribers to read an account like this one.

Discovering these newsletters whetted my curiosity about James Howell. What is Howell's own life story? Where did the energy and courage come from to engage in a project like this in 1971? What happened to all the letters that readers sent in? Are they preserved anywhere? A web search only uncovered a few scattered references to Howell. Will a more substantial collection of papers materialize at some point? I certainly hope so. A fuller and more complete story of him and TVIS deserves to be told.

9

A Mother to Her Family: The Life of Robinn Dupree

Whereas Howell's life combined discretion with a desire to build a strong network among people like himself, some gender-nonconforming individuals put themselves out there, visible to anyone who chose to see. The truth of this was brought home to me when I stumbled upon the small box of papers at the Gerber/Hart Library and Archives labeled "Robinn Dupree."

In November 1996, a professor in folk studies at Western Kentucky University took his class of graduate students to Nashville to see a performance of female impersonators at a bar, the Connection. One of those students, Erin Roth, was so impressed by the event and by the lead performer, Robinn Dupree, that she asked for permission to do her seminar paper not on the assigned project—studies of "riverboat captains and old-time musicians"—but instead to be allowed to interview Dupree and write about the art of female impersonation. The professor said yes, and so Roth conducted two interviews with Dupree, in March and April 1997. Fortunately, she donated the tapes, a typed transcript, and her seminar paper to Gerber/Hart, so that Dupree's account of her own life is now available for inclusion in our collective history.

To summarize her story: Dupree was born in 1952 in Chicago, her mother of Sicilian background and her father a Puerto Rican of Afri-

The research for this essay is based on the Robinn Dupree Papers, Gerber/Hart Library and Archives.

can heritage. When she was in the eighth grade, she told her mother, who taught at a Catholic elementary school, that she was gay. As a teenager, she discovered the Baton Show Lounge, which had just opened on Clark Street in the Near North neighborhood. Destined to become a hallowed institution of the city's LGBTQ community, it was run by Jim Flint, who was already well known for his performances as a female impersonator. Soon she was sneaking out of the house to go there regularly. Sundays were "amateur night" at the Baton, and Dupree took part as often as she could. "It's like I found what I wanted to do," she told Roth. She caught the attention of Flint, and he began coaching her. Soon Dupree was part of the formal entertainment.

Dupree did shows at the Baton for almost a decade, and then moved on to another club, La Cage. In the 1970s, police raids of LGBTQ bars and clubs were still a grim reality. "Any given night it could be this big bust," she recalled. "I experienced it twice." Then, in 1982, her boyfriend of ten years, who had connections to an organized crime syndicate, was killed in a car bombing outside their apartment building. Dupree realized it would be best to leave Chicago quickly, and she resettled in Louisville, Kentucky, where she rapidly made her way into the local female impersonator scene. Over the next decades, she performed for long stretches in Louisville, Nashville, and Indianapolis. According to online sources, her last show before retiring as a performer was on February 13, 2016.

Several themes emerge from Dupree's life story. One involves economics. For those like Dupree who took the work of impersonation seriously as an art form and devoted themselves to it, the economic realities could be harsh. On one hand, costs were high: the dresses, the jewelry, and everything else associated with the glamor of their performance were expensive, and new apparel had to be bought regularly for new shows. On the other hand, wages were low. In the 1970s, working four nights a week, Dupree received twenty-five dollars a night. She and other performers depended on tips, but these were unpredictable and did not always support them sufficiently. Interestingly, Dupree observed that heterosexual audience members were often more appreciative than gays, who tended in her view "to be more prejudiced against drag queens." The irony of this was not lost on her. "We were really the stepping stone for gay people," she told Roth. "We were the first out people."

Thus, most impersonators needed to have a day job, but that brought them up against the gender boundaries of the culture. "You get to this stage," Dupree commented, "where you don't totally look like a man and you don't really look like a woman. So it's hard to get a job." For a stretch of time, she had a job as a receptionist in Evanston, just north of Chicago. But when a gay male employee spread the word that he had seen her on stage as a female impersonator, some women employees started to complain about her use of the women's restroom. Fortunately, another group of women employees came to her defense, but the situation highlighted for Dupree how hard it generally was for people like herself to "make it in society."

Another theme is family. The documentary film *Paris Is Burning* and the television series *Pose* have opened a window to the underground performance world of "ball" culture and the "houses" that sustain it. As Dupree became a well-known, successful, and seasoned performer, younger impersonators-to-be came to her for advice, tutoring, and support, just as she had received from Jim Flint when she was starting and barely out of her teens. To many, she was their "mother," and to Dupree, they were her "daughters." The terms conjure up images of a warm and intimate family of choice, which it is. But behind the pull to use those terms was a harsh reality. After Dupree started performing, her biological mother broke off contact with her, and they remained separated for ten years. "Most people who do drag or want to become women, their family totally disowns them," Dupree told Roth in their interview. Although Dupree acknowledged that much had changed in the twenty-five-plus years since she had started performing, the loss of connection to families of origin remained true for many. Thus, the relationships that were established had significant emotional and practical meaning. Dupree's daughters often lived with her for long stretches as they worked to establish a life for themselves. Yes, it was a chosen family, as the families of many LGBTQ people are, but it was also a deeply needed family.

A third issue emerged from the interview with Dupree: the complexities and shadings of identity. At the time of the interview, in 1997, transgender had just recently established itself as a term of preference in the LGBTQ movement and in activist circles. Dupree described herself as "a pre-operative transsexual . . . I live every day of my life as a woman." She had had surgeries done on her face to accentuate a kind of feminine beauty. She had also done hormone treatments in order to increase her believability as a performer in the world of female impersonation. "That's why I actually ended up taking hormones and becoming a pre-op," she told Roth. "Not to become a woman, but to look as much like a woman on stage as possible." And within this world of stage performance, at least in the decades in which Dupree was an important presence, a range of self-understandings existed. "I have some daughters who want to be just entertainers. Then I have other daughters who want to go all the way through and become a woman."

As I hope this brief account of the life of Robinn Dupree suggests, oral histories offer the promise of preserving limitless treasures of LGBTQ life experience as well as offering insights that will deepen our historical understanding. We need more of them. Go out and interview someone now!

10

Controversy on Campus: Northwestern University and Garrett Theological Seminary

Two of the most important arenas in which LGBTQ activism has played out are religious communities of faith and institutions of higher education. The 1960s were an important decade for both of these institutional settings. College students were major participants in the protests against racial oppression that filled the decade, and campuses saw militant mass action against US war-making in Southeast Asia. The student generation of the 1960s also came to symbolize the sexual revolution, whose reverberations have continued to affect American politics ever since. Meanwhile, the deep involvement of religious leaders in the African American civil rights movement as well as in the peace movement meant that many communities of faith found themselves engaged in debate about some of the most pressing and controversial issues of the day.

This questioning of old truths and challenging of institutional order also extended to the topic of homosexuality. Even before the Stonewall Uprising of 1969 ushered in a new era of militant activism, San Francisco saw the formation of a Council on Religion and the Homosexual. It brought together ministers from several Christian denominations with LGBTQ activists and fostered a dialogue that led to new activist initiatives. And, as protests became commonplace on campuses, the first student groups, which described

The research for this essay is based on the Samuel Todes Papers, Gerber/Hart Library and Archives.

themselves as "homophile" organizations, were formed at a few universities in the second half of the sixties. With the birth of gay liberation after Stonewall, both religious and campus activism took off. The number of groups multiplied quickly. They provoked debates within many religions about the morality of same-sex relations and the place of LGBTQ people in their communities. And campus activists across the country demanded recognition and funding for their student groups as well as support for research and inclusion within the curriculum.

Much of the time, these two areas of activism remained unconnected. But, in 1978, they intersected in highly visible ways in Evanston, Illinois, just north of Chicago, at the linked campuses of Northwestern University and Garrett-Evangelical Theological Seminary. On April 12, 1978, two students at Garrett wrote a coming out letter that they made public. James Mason and Terry Colbert met as first-year students at the seminary in the previous fall. They quickly fell in love. "To all who are interested," their letter began, "we publicly acknowledge our homosexual partnership." They recognized that this declaration might jeopardize their hopes of becoming ministers in the United Methodist Church, but they were unwilling to propagate the dishonesty that silence involved. To their religious colleagues, both faculty and staff, they put forward the idea that "it is still possible that what the world takes for evil, God has intended for good."

The 1976 *Discipline of the United Methodist Church*, which laid out core beliefs and institutional practices for the denomination, said that homosexuals were "persons of sacred worth." But at the same time, it unambiguously stated that "we do not condone the practice of homosexuality and consider this practice incompatible with Christian teaching." Not surprisingly, such a theological stance "precludes the ordination of self-proclaimed homosexuals." On May 15, a month after Mason and Colbert wrote their letter, the faculty at Garrett voted not to "advance them" to the next stage of the program in which they were enrolled. Mason and Colbert were, in effect, expelled from Garrett Theological for coming out as gay.

At the same time, the faculty explicitly voted to bar "self-declared homosexuals" from all of Garrett's professional degree programs.

The actions taken by the faculty at Garrett did not sit well with many at Northwestern, and voices of dissent quickly made themselves heard. James Avery, the chaplain at Northwestern, gave a sermon on campus the Sunday after the Garrett vote. Boldly titling it "Queer Things," Avery walked his audience through the various antigay readings of Scripture and emphasized "the serious disputes even among experts." The faculty's decision at Garrett, he said, "angers me." Calling them and others "our contemporary Pharisees," he forthrightly condemned "the hysterical arguments of those who rationalize their own intrinsic hatred of homosexuality."

Avery was just the first to speak up. Others followed. In an open letter to faculty at Garrett, William Earle, a professor of philosophy, declared that "your recent decision caused something of a *shock* among civilized, educated, and moral people." Samuel Todes, who was the faculty advisor to GALA, the student Gay and Lesbian Alliance on the Northwestern University campus, was especially visible in his response to Garrett. Writing to high-level officials in the Northwestern administration, he described the "unjustified intimidation" that many students were feeling after the Garrett decision. "Northwestern has to make *its* stand equally clear, that sexual orientation is *not* a criterion for the admission of students or the hiring of faculty." If it doesn't, he continued, Northwestern should expect to face a major "media event" in the fall.

Debate and discussion continued over the next year. At Garrett, the Women's Concerns Committee held a weekend seminar on homosexuality in which, among other sessions, they invited Mason and Colbert to speak. Charles Mehler, a graduate student who was active at Northwestern in campus governance, urged the university to "sever all reciprocal and mutual agreements" with Garrett and demanded that the board of trustees "censures [Garrett] for this deplorable inhuman action." The student government condemned the dismissal. The *Daily Northwestern*, the campus newspaper, covered the controversy extensively and was unambiguous in its criticism of

Garrett as it urged Northwestern "to make its counterweight felt." By the autumn, the issue was receiving mainstream news coverage. A headline in the *Chicago Sun-Times* declared, "Northwestern University Faculty Rips Dismissal of Gays at Garrett."

Todes himself was a key player in this ongoing debate. Because of his role as advisor to GALA, he had a great deal more contact with queer students than most faculty at that time. He began to organize a protest petition among those Northwestern faculty who found themselves engaged in cooperative activities with Garrett, such as teaching courses that Garrett students enrolled in or sitting on dissertation committees. Of the sixty-three faculty at Northwestern with such connections to Garrett, Todes had gotten signatures from forty-eight who agreed to sever such ties unless Garrett reversed itself.

So how did all of this turn out? The results were, at best, mixed. On the positive side, it did cause a year of significant debate, thus creating a much higher level of visibility for LGBTQ issues at Northwestern. It led to the appointment of a committee that, in spring 1979, produced a twelve-page "Report of the Committee on Gay and Lesbian Life at Northwestern University." Among the recommendations that were implemented was the funding of the Gay and Lesbian Alliance. On the anniversary of Colbert's and Mason's dismissal, students at Northwestern organized a service of remembrance on the front lawn of Garrett. Meanwhile, a Northwestern faculty report declared that Garrett's position would remain "an irritant in the relationship between Garrett and Northwestern." Some faculty did, in fact, stop working on cooperative efforts. But Northwestern did not sever its ties with the theological seminary, and the campaign to have Garrett change its policies failed. In 2016, the *Discipline of the United Methodist Church* continued to declare that "self-avowed practicing homosexuals are not to be certified as candidates, ordained as ministers, or appointed to serve in The United Methodist Church." And, in 2019, at its General Conference held in Saint Louis, a majority of representatives voted to sustain the ban on performing marriages for same-sex couples and on ordaining LGBTQ candidates for the ministry.

And what of Terry Colbert and James Mason? A year after their dismissal, an article in the *Daily Northwestern* reported that they were living together in Champaign, Illinois. Colbert was getting a graduate degree in English at the University of Illinois, and Mason worked in a library. They both remained outspoken gay activists, each of them serving as an advisor to the student group on campus and regularly speaking to church congregations about gay liberation. A public letter that they wrote in June 1979 captures well their views on their action: "The choice we made for the side of truth and love has brought us greater happiness than we had ever known . . . A life without love . . . is a walking death."

11

Activist Catholics: Dignity's Work in the 1970s and 1980s

Before the 1960s, the Roman Catholic Church was like every other Christian community of faith. Homosexuality was a sin. Some denominations may have incorporated medical frameworks into their language, but there was little evidence of a significant move toward acceptance and approval. That started to change very slowly in the 1960s as a few church activists and reformers began to speak out in support of gays and lesbians. This tendency to press for change accelerated in the 1970s and 1980s. Several religious denominations began to revisit official teachings on homosexuality and open themselves up to acceptance of LGBTQ members.

The Roman Catholic Church, however, stood out as moving distinctly against the grain. In October 1986, with the approval of Pope John Paul II, Cardinal Ratzinger issued a "Letter to the Bishops of the Catholic Church on the Pastoral Care of Homosexuals." For many who had been raised Catholic but felt compelled to leave the church because of its moral condemnation, the document offered no surprises. Ratzinger's letter took a strong and uncompromising stand against any expression of homosexuality. It described homosexual behavior as "an intrinsic moral evil" and a homosexual orientation as "an objective disorder." In posing the question as to whether being a sexually active gay man was "a morally acceptable

The research for this essay is based on the Jim Bussen Papers, Gerber/Hart Library and Archives.

option," it offered a categorically unambiguous answer: "It is not." This 1986 document reinforced the image of Roman Catholicism as unremittingly, inflexibly, and eternally homophobic. There seemed to be no possibility of change. And when Cardinal Ratzinger became Pope Benedict in 2005, it only confirmed this perspective.

The papers of James Bussen in Gerber/Hart's archives suggest the need for a more nuanced history of the Catholic response to gay and lesbian activism in the post-Stonewall era than what I have just described. Bussen was a longtime, prominent Chicago activist who, in the early 1970s, was a founder of the local Dignity chapter. Dignity was for decades the primary organization giving voice to LGBTQ Catholics. Bussen remained continuously involved in the organization and later served as its national president in the second half of the 1980s.

The documentation that Bussen amassed in his work made it abundantly clear to me that one of the effects of Ratzinger's 1986 letter was to erase from my historical memory, and I suspect from the memory of many others as well, a rich history of LGBTQ activism within the Catholic Church in the US in the 1970s and early 1980s. At the simplest level, Dignity grew as an organization with impressive speed. Founded right at the beginning of the 1970s in the wake of the energy released by Stonewall and the birth of gay liberation, it expanded from seven chapters in 1973 to eighty-one by 1979. And its chapters did not primarily exist in the large urban areas often associated with LGBTQ communities. By the end of the decade, Dignity was a presence in such places as Lubbock, Texas; Cheyenne, Wyoming; Sioux City, Iowa; and Birmingham, Alabama. Given how new gay liberation still was in the 1970s and how it was struggling for broad national visibility, Dignity chapters in these smaller communities must have been a precious resource. They created and sustained connections among people who often were still largely in "the closet" and were likely to be relatively isolated. When Dignity held its third biennial convention in Chicago in 1977, 430 people registered for the national gathering of an organization that had already grown to four thousand members. That was exceptionally large for an LGBTQ organization in the 1970s. No explicitly political LGBTQ organization had that many members during these years.

But Dignity's significance in these years was not only about its size. Dignity projected a strong message of confidence and militancy. In its May 1973 newsletter, the editor wrote: "A force is growing within the Church. It will not be stopped." At the end of the decade, the newsletter directed these words to its members: "it will not be theologians sitting in their offices who will one day decide that homosexuality makes sense . . . theologians will come around to thinking that *only* after a good number of gay people have already made sense of their own lives." In other words, come out. Show your pride by how you live and what you do.

The church, too, was responding in encouraging ways. In 1976, the Young Adult Ministry of the US Catholic Conference issued a very positive statement about gay men and lesbians. "The Church must be with gay men and women, learn from them, and be their advocates," it declared. At the local level, Dignity found itself in dialogue with a number of the more liberal Catholic bishops. Also in 1976, Dignity received an invitation to attend the "Call to Action" Conference of the Catholic Church in the US. The conference passed the following resolution: "That the Church actively seek to serve the pastoral needs of those persons with a homosexual orientation; to root out those structures and attitudes which discriminate against homosexuals as persons; and to join the struggle by homosexual men and women for their basic constitutional rights to employment, housing, and immigration." Brian McNaught, who attended the conference and has remained an activist in this arena for more than four decades, wrote of the meeting that "Dignity was in its finest hour."

The gay-positive quality of the conference statement provides a necessary context for the 1986 letter by Cardinal Ratzinger. Rather than a simple articulation of the standard teachings of Catholicism, Ratzinger's missive represented an aggressive assault upon serious grassroots efforts that were stirring things up and provoking progressive change. From the late 1970s into the 1980s, Dignity chapters around the country were pushing hard for acceptance and inclusion and were making noteworthy progress. In 1979, Dignity's national officers met with a group of bishops from the National Catholic Conference and afterward described the meeting as "very productive." At their annual banquet in 1980, the Association of Priests of the Archdiocese of Chicago honored Dignity as their "Organization of the Year." Priests participated in the celebration of Mass at Dignity conferences around the US.

The 1986 letter by Cardinal Ratzinger did, of course, represent a concerted effort from the top of the Catholic Church hierarchy to end these developments. And it does assuredly mark a turning point away from the liberalization and inclusion that seemed to be happening. After 1986, bishops across the US began to deny Dignity chapters use of church facilities. But the Ratzinger statement and the response of bishops did not signal an immediate end to LGBTQ activism by Dignity. Bussen and other national officers pushed back. In a March 1987 letter to Bishop John May of Saint Louis, who was president of the National Conference of Catholic Bishops, Bussen described "a continuing pattern of discrimination against Dignity chapters and the use and abuse of facts and myths about AIDS by the Church." The next month, Bussen met with Bishop May to discuss Dignity's grievances. Bussen felt that May was surprisingly responsive and that the bishop "strongly reaffirmed" a commitment to minister to gays and lesbians.

Jim Bussen's papers left me with a very strong sense that there is much to be learned by researching the history of Catholic LGBTQ activism and the church's response in the 1970s and 1980s. Some of Bussen's materials will prove very valuable to that project. The collection includes a file of copies of *Dignity: A National Publication*, stretching from 1972 to 1987, and two unpublished documents, "Dignity: A Brief History, 1969-1981," and "Dignity/USA 25: A Chronology, 1969-1994." Without doubt, there is a book waiting to be written.

12

Dennis Halan and the Story of Chicago's "Gay Mass"

As I suggested in the essay about Dignity's work to achieve change within the Catholic Church, researching history can disrupt one's assumptions about the past and its trajectory of change. What I learned from the work of James Bussen and Dignity propelled me to search for more stories about a religion-focused activism. The experience of Dennis Halan, one of the earliest—perhaps, even, *the* earliest—LGBTQ religious activist in Chicago, offered even more surprises about how such work came together in the first decade after Stonewall.

The documents that Halan gave to Gerber/Hart are rich in detail about how something called "the Gay Mass" came into being and how it grew and evolved over the succeeding three years. In 1970, Halan was involved in the Chicago Gay Alliance, the activist group that had just broken off from Chicago Gay Liberation. CGA was holding its meetings on West Elm Street in the Near North neighborhood. On September 17, a woman named Mary Houlihan addressed a meeting of the alliance. Houlihan was a leader of the Legion of Mary, a Catholic women's organization that reached out to marginalized groups, provided them with services, and arranged for special Masses to be held. The Legion worked with homeless youth, incarcerated women, and alcoholics, among others, and that summer,

The research for this essay is based on the Dennis Halan Papers, Gerber/Hart Library and Archives.

probably because of the new visibility that gay liberation activism was creating, the Legion had begun a "homosexual ministry." Houlihan came to CGA to recruit volunteers for the Legion's work. As Halan recounted, "it was Mary Houlihan's thought that if homosexuals wanted rights and acceptance from strait [sic] people, it might be in their best interest to do volunteer work with strait people. Like a give and take. Straits would be more accepting to gay people."

Houlihan's proposal, according to Halan, "turned me and the others off." But her description of the Masses that the Legion arranged pushed Halan to turn the meeting around by asking Houlihan "why don't you have Masses for gay people?" She admitted that she had never thought of it, but was suddenly intrigued. Several other Legion people had come to the CGA meeting, including a Franciscan priest, "Father Max." Halan asked him directly whether he would be willing to say such a Mass, and Father Max agreed that, if Halan could find at least several others committed to attending such an event, he would officiate. Halan immediately surveyed the CGA members who were present, and twenty-five of them expressed interest.

But would it happen? Halan was passionate about it from the moment the idea came to him. "I wouldn't let this go," he wrote. "I didn't want this to be a concept only—but an action." He stayed in touch with Houlihan and won her commitment to help. After much searching, he found a friend, Wayne Evans, who lived in a neighborhood, Lakeview, that gay men were starting to gather in and who was willing to let his apartment at 642 West Aldine be the setting for the Mass. And so, on a Wednesday night, October 14, the first of what would commonly be referred to as the "Gay Mass" was held. Twelve attended, evenly divided between women and men. Facing the group of celebrants and dressed in gold brocade vestments, Father Max said the Mass in English, which was becoming increasingly common practice at that time. "I felt like an early Christian with that small, intimate group of people," Halan recalled.

The Mass had a history that stretched out over several years, the same years in which Catholic LGBTQ activism was going across the United States. At first it met once a month. In February 1971, Cardinal John Cody, the leader of the Chicago Catholic archdiocese, learned about the Mass and immediately ordered Father Robert Behman to stop officiating (apparently "Father Max" was how he was known on the streets by the people the Legion of Mary served). An unsigned document titled "Out of the Catacombs, Into the Streets" condemned "the arbitrary whims of a man nationally known for his indifferent and callous contempt for the rights of minority groups in the Chicago area." The Chicago Gay Alliance debated whether to start picketing outside Holy Name Cathedral to protest the cardinal's action, but Halan and others attending the Mass asked CGA to wait. Two months later, the cardinal gave permission for Father Behman to continue saying the Mass, but he also specified that it not be advertised in mainstream media. The Mass was said on Tuesdays, twice a month, still in private homes. In September 1971, Saint Sebastian, a Catholic church in Lakeview on Wellington Street, just off Halsted, began hosting the biweekly Mass. An article in the CGA newsletter of October 1971 reported on the transition to Saint Sebastian, which it praised. But because the services were held on Tuesday, the writer described them as "only a snack, not the main meal. The Gay is only a stepchild."

By the time of the move to Saint Sebastian, an average of thirty-five or so individuals were attending each Mass. The shift to a church increased participation; sixty-five attended the first anniversary service in October. Finally, with the cardinal's permission, the first Sunday Mass occurred in May 1972. Halan and other regulars expected that the shift away from Tuesdays to Sunday, which was a day of obligatory Mass attendance for Catholics, would likely double or even triple regular attendance, and in fact by that summer the numbers had noticeably grown.

Meanwhile, the organizational context for the Gay Mass was shifting. The Chicago Gay Alliance never had much interest in it, and so Houlihan and Halan formed a new organization, Unity. It did the work of keeping the Mass going, reaching out to potential attendees, and organizing rap groups and other activities. Even though the content of the work was primarily religious, Unity also had an activist edge to it, in that it was at least implicitly, and sometimes explicitly, challenging traditional Catholic views. For instance, in a talk Father Max gave to the assembled group, he declared that "there are no scriptural laws against homosexuality." He went on to say the church was "undergoing changes. The certitudes are gone. So you can be a Christian and engage in homosexual activity."

Chicagoans were also reaching out to religious activists elsewhere. Halan had heard about Dignity, the organization of LGBTQ Catholics that had formed in San Diego late in 1969 and was spreading to other cities. Dignity saw itself as activist as well as religious. An editorial in its newsletter from June 1971 proclaimed: "It is time now to come out of the closets, to quit running, to take a stand and fight, to give time and talent where possible. It is time to become informed. It is time to be proud. Yes, the Church bears much blame for the plight of gays. But, so does the gay himself. And if the Church has a responsibility to correct injustices, so much the more does the gay himself have the responsibility to speak up and work for acceptance."

Before long, some of those attending the Mass formed a Chicago Dignity chapter. The connection to a larger organization with national aspirations brought the Gay Mass more press attention, with the *Chicago Sun-Times* running an article about it. It also brought renewed censure from Cardinal Cody. Though he didn't order it to stop, he did once again demand that organizers of it stop seeking publicity and promoting it through the press.

The formation of the Dignity chapter seems to have engendered conflict between it and Unity, although none of the documents in Halan's papers explicitly address the reasons why. By the end of 1973, Unity seems to have faded from the scene. One development that did generate commentary was a noteworthy one. With Dignity's taking responsibility for the Mass by the summer of 1972, the identity of those attending changed. "The young gays," the author noted, "were the first to respond and were responsible for its success." Dignity attracted an older, middle-aged group of gay men to the Mass, and before long the youth and the lesbians seem to have disappeared.

Despite these changes, Dignity remained a strong and visible presence in Chicago at least into the 1980s and perhaps beyond as well. The Gay Mass was still being held at Saint Sebastian in the fall of 1979, nine years after it began and eight years after Saint Sebastian opened its doors to it. As to its significance for those who made it happen, a postscript that Halan added to his handwritten account captures it well: "It is very important to note that twenty-eight years ago, homosexuals and lesbians were vilified and not talked about . . . That's why to start a Roman Catholic Mass for the homosexual and lesbian community was so courageous. It went against the religious and social fabric of its time. To start the Mass was one thing, to keep it another."

13

Moving Forward with Integrity

As I hope the essays on Dignity and on the Gay Mass in Chicago have demonstrated, there is a vibrant, energetic history of LGBTQ religious activism. The first bits of religious activism began in the two decades before Stonewall, during the "homophile" phase of the movement. But after the birth of a radical and militant gay liberation movement in 1969, organizing by activists within communities of faith expanded at a phenomenal rate. This growth and its impact come through clearly in the work of Integrity, an organization of LGBTQ Episcopalians.

Perhaps the first thing to emerge from the history of Integrity is the importance of individual initiative. In the case of Integrity, the role of Louie Crew stands out. Crew began teaching English at Fort Valley State College in Georgia in 1973. He was among the first cohort of academics to come out and to do intellectual work related to homosexuality. He attended the second annual conference of the Gay Academic Union, held in New York over Thanksgiving weekend in 1974; presented a paper on the writer Christopher Isherwood at the Modern Language Association's convention the following month; and was a member of the Gay Caucus that had already formed in the MLA. As if being an out-of-the-closet faculty member in Fort Valley, Georgia, in the mid-1970s was not challeng-

The research for this essay is based on the records of Integrity, Gerber/Hart Library and Archives.

65

ing enough, he also founded Integrity and began publishing a national newsletter in November 1974. This bundle of activist energy produced a newsletter every month that, in those years, required him to come up with content that either he or others whom he recruited wrote, and then to type, duplicate, maintain a name and address list, and mail the hard-copy issues to his steadily growing list of subscribers.

The early issues of the newsletter make it evident that the time was right for Crew to take this initiative. In January 1973 the Episcopal House of Bishops had convened a Task Force on Homophiles and the Ministry. It had already met several times when Crew commenced with his newsletter, and one can assume that the conversations and correspondence that the task force generated created the initial networks that he used to publicize Integrity and circulate the publication. By the time of the fourth issue, he was able to report that a Chicago chapter of Integrity had already formed and that groups were convening in New York, Atlanta, Cincinnati, and Washington, DC. "Local and regional chapters are springing up all over," he reported with enthusiasm. By summer, membership had surpassed three hundred, and, just a year after Crew mailed out his first newsletter, there were twenty chapters in fifteen states.

A key activity of Integrity was the national convention that it held each year, starting in the summer of 1975 in Chicago. These annual gatherings, which met in a different city each August, were vital to the growth of the organization. Half a century after Stonewall and the birth of gay liberation, it can be hard to imagine how revolutionary a large open gathering of gays and lesbians would have seemed in the mid-1970s to almost all the participants. In those years, when LGBTQ people got together, it tended to be in the private intimacy of a house party or in a bar, which carried the lurking danger of a police raid and arrests. Pride Marches were happening only in a small number of cities and were tending to attract at best a few thousand people. The Integrity conventions allowed participants to feel that they were part of something big. Rooms vibrated with energy and excitement as notable speakers challenged the theological condemnation of homosexual expression. Activists from different cities described what they were doing on the ground to move the Episcopal Church to change its teachings and provide a welcoming and accepting environment for its gay and lesbian members.

Crew made it clear in his newsletter that a publication alone was not enough to spark the change that needed to happen. "There also needs to be a local, visible organization," he wrote in August 1975, "because we are, willy nilly, going to have to confront and struggle and knock heads with a local visible organization in the form of parish churches and dioceses, with homophobic priests and bishops . . . Our claim is that we have a right to be here; most of the Church rejects that claim out of hand . . . There will be a long fight ahead."

The Chicago Integrity newsletter gives a sense of what local chapters could do. Almost immediately after its founding in January 1975, Jim Wickcliff, the president of the chapter, sent to the rector of every Episcopalian congregation in the Chicago metropolitan area a copy of "Christian Words to a Homosexual," the text of a sermon by Norman Pittenger, a pro-gay theologian. Wickcliff also informed local congregations that members of Integrity were willing to visit their parish and offer lectures and discussions on gay life, the gay movement, and the developing movement for acceptance within the church. Several Chicago members appeared on Phil Donahue's nationally syndicated television talk show. Wickcliff and others worked with local activists trying to get antidiscrimination legislation passed by the city; they sought endorsements of the legislation from Episcopalian ministers. And Chicago's chapter was not alone in this kind of activist activity. In Michigan, for example, Integrity activists recruited a minister to testify in a lesbian mother's child custody case. The diocese in Michigan had issued a positive report on homosexuality, and the lawyer in the case was able to submit it as part of the evidence supporting the mother's effort to maintain custody of her child. Investigating the activity of Integrity chapters across the US is likely to reveal a rich history of such local activism on a wide variety of LGBTQ issues.

One element of Integrity's history that particularly caught my attention involved the role of lesbians in the organization. A major thread in the history of the 1970s was the recurring tension between gay men and lesbians. On one hand, it expressed itself in the demands of lesbians for fair representation in the leadership and programming of an organization; on the other, it often led to a bitter parting of the ways as the sexism of many gay men proved intolerable. A somewhat different picture emerges for Integrity in the 1970s. Crew seems to have made a concerted effort to recruit women into visible leadership roles. He brought Ellen Barrett on as an associate editor of the national newsletter, and she made a point of soliciting writing from lesbians and occasionally devoting an entire issue to women's place in the church. Integrity also established a "co-presidency" and a "co-vice-presidency" with one man and one woman in each role. Kate Jones, who filled the vice-presidency role for a time in the mid-1970s, wrote in one of the newsletter issues "Is Integrity for a woman? Will it help me find wholeness and live responsibly in community? This woman answers, 'yes.'"

Yet, at the same time, Barrett put out the challenges that lesbians faced. "We must be a voice for ourselves as women before we can hope to be heard intelligently as gays," she wrote in an editorial. "Few of us are likely to be able to afford the inevitable energy-draining effort of fighting a two-front war . . . The initial work . . . will have to be a mostly male effort." At a certain point, Barrett found herself having to act on that assessment. Without any bitterness toward the men in Integrity, she announced her resignation. Barrett, who had a history of activism in the Daughters of Bilitis in the late 1960s and then in the Gay Liberation Front and Radicalesbians in the early 1970s, had entered General Theological Seminary to study for a master of divinity degree. She became a key figure in the movement to allow for the ordination of women, and in September 1976, the General Convention of the Episcopal Church approved it. Ordained in January 1977 by Bishop Paul Moore in New York, Barrett was among the first forty women ordained. But, more importantly, she openly identified as a lesbian, making her the first lesbian and only the second acknowledged LGBTQ minister in any Christian denomination. As Crew wrote in the February newsletter, Barrett's ordination "has set off an expected firestorm of protest: the Pharisees are rending their garments and squealing like stuck pigs."

As Crew's description suggests, Integrity members were not reticent about calling out the homophobia of church officials. But it was just this kind of overt militancy that was necessary to move Christian denominations out of a historical tradition of intolerance that had lasted for centuries.

14

Lutherans Concerned: A Continuing Struggle

With Chicago's large and diverse population, a diversity reflected in the wide range of religious affiliation among its residents, it makes sense that LGBTQ Chicagoans sustained several religious-oriented organizations in the 1970s and 1980s. Besides Dignity and Integrity, there was also a chapter of Lutherans Concerned. Its collection in the Gerber/Hart archives captures both the broad national reach of its work as well as the passion that activists brought to the effort to make faith communities accepting of their queer members.

Lutherans Concerned formed in Minneapolis in June 1974 at a gathering that brought together activists from across the country. Already by that time, just five years after the Stonewall Uprising had launched a gay liberation movement, nine other religious faiths had caucuses of LGBTQ members. The two individuals chosen as co-ordinators of Lutherans Concerned were Diane Fraser and Allen Blaich. Fraser was a thirty-one-year-old instructor in sociology at Gustavus Adolphus College, a Lutheran-affiliated school in small-town Minnesota; she lived in the countryside on a farm with her female lover. Blaich was a twenty-three-year-old college student at the University of Utah. A native of North Dakota, he attended services of the LGBTQ-oriented Metropolitan Community Church in Salt Lake City. An experienced activist, Blaich was already serving

The research for this essay is based on the records of Lutherans Concerned/North America, Gerber/Hart Library and Archives.

on the national council of the Lutheran Student Movement and was head of its Committee on Homosexuality.

Lutherans Concerned released the first issue of its newsletter, the *Gay Lutheran*, a month after its founding, and the newsletter gives a sense of the stance of the founders. "We Confront Church," the headline on its front page announced. "Our church has misled, misunderstood, confused, alienated, and unjustly condemned us," the article forthrightly declared. It promised that Lutherans Concerned would serve as "a rallying point for gay and lay people, to provide a visible gay identity the church can no longer ignore." Among the founding members were representatives from all three of the major Lutheran denominations—the American Lutheran Church, the Lutheran Church in America, and the Missouri Synod.

Organizing as openly gay and lesbian among Lutherans took courage in this era, since all three denominations were overt in their condemnation. A 1966 report of the American Lutheran Church had described same-sex relationships as "warped." The president of the Lutheran Church in America characterized homosexuality as "a departure from God's heterosexual order." In 1973, the year before Lutherans Concerned formed, Robert Marshall, the president of the Missouri Synod, had rejected a request to affirm gay and lesbian congregants and instead declared homosexuality sinful. Lutheran Church in America officials in Philadelphia allied with the Roman Catholic hierarchy there to oppose a proposed gay rights bill before the city council. The desire to preserve a distance from the work of Lutherans Concerned was manifested in the refusal of the official publications of all three denominations to acknowledge its formation, despite the fact that mainstream press organs, like the *Minneapolis Star*, the *Detroit News*, and the *Salt Lake City Tribune*, had written stories about it. Efforts to place paid ads in church publications were repeatedly rejected.

Despite this, the activists at the center of Lutherans Concerned found ways to put their message out. Both Fraser and Blaich attended the annual conference of the Lutheran Student Movement and the Lutheran Campus Pastors in 1974 and were given an opportunity to speak. They showed a short documentary film, *A Position of Faith*, on the ordination of Bill Johnson, an openly gay pastoral student, by the United Church of Christ. As Fraser commented later, "There wasn't a dry eye in the house." Late in 1974, Blaich and another Lutherans Concerned activist, Marie Kent, who was from Minneapolis, appeared at the biennial convention of American Lutheran Church, which was held in Detroit. Putting aside their militant rhetoric, they maintained "a low-key presence" in the hope of "winning new friends to the cause of gay justice in the church." Staffing an information booth, Blaich and Kent distributed hundreds of brochures that described the mission of Lutherans Concerned and the challenges that gay and lesbian Lutherans faced. Over the course of several days, a number of delegates revealed in confidence that they were gay. Many others quietly expressed support. Reflecting on the experience, Blaich and Kent wrote that "we were amazed to discover just how many friends the gay Lutheran has within the church's colleges, agencies and parishes."

"Coming out," a key pillar of the post-Stonewall movement, was central to the ability of Lutherans Concerned to pursue its mission of winning acceptance. The first issue of its newsletter put out a call for "*active* members." Marie Kent, one of the core organizers, wrote that "we need to stand tall and declare that we are not ashamed of who we are." Yet, in the mid-1970s, it was easier to issue the call than it was for many Lutherans to accept it. The *Gay Lutheran* was open to recognizing this. Its issues contain several touching stories from pastors of congregations who, although in the closet, were willing to write about themselves under pseudonyms like "Pastor D" and "Pastor X." Their autobiographical accounts gave substance to the claim that the negative stance of Lutheran denominations toward homosexuality extracted a heavy price. As "Mr. A" argued, "for many gay pastors or other gay officials in church agencies, to come out publicly would mean the end of their career, their life's work in the church. Other gay Lutherans have not yet built up the emotional inner strength to take the plunge." He affirmed the critical need for "openly gay Lutherans," but also argued that "just as vitally we need the efforts of every other gay Lutheran as well." Even those who weren't out "can still be an active part of Lutherans Concerned."

Throughout the 1970s, Lutherans Concerned maintained a dynamic presence at the local level. Chapters were quickly established in a number of cities; Chicago's was among the first three that formed. By 1978, there were almost two dozen scattered across the United States. Lutherans Concerned members made contact with pastors of local congregations known to have a generally liberal outlook on social justice issues. "Supportive ministries have increased markedly in Lutheran circles," the Gay Lutheran reported in its May-June 1976 issue. That same month the steering committee of Lutherans Concerned issued a "Gay Ministry Statement," which was designed to offer direction to pastors and congregations on how to treat their gay and lesbian members. It displayed a similar optimism. "The doors of Lutheran parishes which have opened wide to gay Christians have been one of the more inspiring features of the 1970s," it declared. "Pastors have evidenced a new willingness to welcome warmly every member of the community." A survey conducted among Missouri Synod Lutherans showed that more than half wished the church would accept gay people. Lutherans Concerned applauded the "large and growing body of support for our cause." Two years later, in 1978, it was still evincing a hopefulness about the prospects of institutional change. On the eve of its first national convention, scheduled to meet in Milwaukee in July 1978, Howard Erickson, then the national coordinator of the group, issued a statement in which he asserted that "1978 is an awfully good time to be gay and to be Christian." With organizations of other LGBTQ Christian groups convening nationally as well, the members of Lutherans Concerned could see themselves as part of a larger movement within the religious world.

The undeniable sense of local progress, however, did not translate into formal institutional change at the national level. The leadership of the major Lutheran denominations resisted calls to conduct formal theological studies that might reevaluate their long-standing tradition of condemnation. Finally, in 1983, the Lutheran Church in America appointed an Advisory Committee of Issues Related to Homosexuality. The report the committee released three years later seemed to walk a very fine line. It made statements suggesting that all humans were equal in God's eyes, that no one group could be singled out "as especially sinful." It described as "striking" that "so few passages exist" in the Bible on homosexuality, and that the Sodom story "leads to less than conclusive results." Theological investigation led the authors to conclude that "we are left finally with conflicting schools of thought . . . The advisory committee is convinced that this church can neither condemn, nor ignore, nor praise and affirm, homosexuality." Rather than propose changes in the Lutheran Church in America's stance on homosexuality, it recommended that a more comprehensive assessment of the issue be authorized. While the Lutherans Concerned collection at Gerber/Hart contains a copy of this report, it does not have documents revealing the discussions that went on among the committee's members or the communications they engaged in with church officials. Such documentation might offer revealing insights into the internal debates among the leadership of the Lutheran Church in America in the mid-1980s.

Lutherans Concerned, meanwhile, continued its activities at the local level. The same year that the Advisory Committee was formed, Lutherans Concerned created a "Reconciled-in-Christ" initiative whose goal was to identify local congregations that welcomed lesbians and gays and included them fully in the sacramental life of the church. One of the very first congregations to sign on was Resurrection Lutheran Church, located in the Chicago neighborhood of Lakeview, which was rapidly becoming the city's most visible "gayborhood." For years, Resurrection had been allowing the Chicago chapter to hold its meetings there. But three years after the reconciling program was launched, there were only twenty-five congregations across the United States participating in the initiative. While the leadership of Lutherans Concerned acknowledged that "some progress" was being made and "small steps" toward acceptance were occurring, they also had to recognize that, more than a decade after they began organizing, "the official stance of the major Lutheran churches maintains that homosexuality is sinful."

The story of Lutherans Concerned confirms a view of the 1970s as a period of widespread dynamic activism in the LGBTQ movement. That activism did bring constructive change in the shape and practice of some local Lutheran congregations, like Resurrection in Chicago. But the effort to bring major formal policy changes at the national level faced deep resistance throughout the 1980s, a resistance that local activists were not able to overcome. It was not until 2009 that the American Lutheran Church and the Lutheran Church in America, which by then had merged into a single denomination, approved the ordination of gay men and lesbians. That decision then led over six hundred conservative congregations to secede from the national body and confirmed that, in some cases, institutional change comes slowly and at a price.

15

Running for Office: The Campaign of Gary Nepon

Within any movement that challenges deep structural oppression, there is likely to be fierce debate about how to achieve change. One wing of a movement, usually described as "radical," will argue that the system is so corrupt and unjust that one cannot play by its rules. Instead, protest is seen as the key avenue for creating change. By making the system unworkable, by paralyzing it through marches, rallies, sit-ins, and other such tactics, these activists hope to force change from normally recalcitrant political structures. Needless to say, these disruptive tactics often receive the greatest attention from media and are thus most closely associated with movements for social change. But, at the same time, most movements also have a wing that attempts to build influence within the political system. They register voters, endorse candidates, propose specific pieces of legislation, and lobby for their passage. Thus, a key question that any movement faces is how to bring these different approaches together. How can protest and electoral politics strengthen each other and thus create a more powerful force for change? As Bayard Rustin argued in "From Protest to Politics," a 1965 appeal to radical activists in the black freedom struggle, ultimate success requires that a movement engage with the political system rather than always remain on the outside.

The research for this essay is based on the Gary Nepon Papers, Gerber/Hart Library and Archives.

For identity-based movements, one form that electoral involvement has taken is running for public office. The first explicitly LGBTQ
electoral campaign that I am aware of happened in 1961 in San Francisco, when José Sarria, a well-known and dearly beloved drag performer at the Black Cat, one of the city's popular bars, ran for the board
of supervisors in response to intense police harassment of LGBTQ
people. But Sarria's campaign was an isolated one-of-a-kind effort.

Most activists in the gay liberation era of the early 1970s did not
put much emphasis on electoral politics. Instead, they were calling
on ordinary folks to come out of the closet. They were marching in
the street. They were disrupting press conferences of public officials. The likelihood that anyone openly gay or lesbian might actually get elected was relatively slim. There were a few notable excep-
tions: Elaine Noble in Massachusetts, Karen Clark and Allan Spear
in Minnesota, and Harvey Milk in San Francisco. But, overall, electoral politics was on the margins of activist consciousness in the first
years after Stonewall.

And then, in 1977, there was the Dade County, Florida, disas-
ter. In January, the county commission passed a sexual orientation
nondiscrimination ordinance. Almost immediately, opponents
launched a campaign to repeal it through a ballot referendum. The
figure most closely associated with the campaign was Anita Bryant, a former beauty queen and popular singer who was the public
face of the Florida citrus industry. Bryant and the repeal campaign
brought greater media attention to the politics of sexual orientation
than anything previously. When voters by a large margin repealed
the ordinance in June, it highlighted the importance of electoral politics as one aspect of movement activism.

This played out in Chicago in an unexpected way. In 1977–78,
Gary Nepon became the first "out" LGBTQ candidate to run in Chicago for a seat in the Illinois state legislature. His experience provides a view of how complex the relationship between a movement
and electoral politics can be. In the fall of 1977, Nepon began putting a campaign together to win a place on the ballot as a candidate
for the Illinois State Assembly from the Thirteenth District on Chi-

cago's North Side lakefront. The district was already in the process of becoming identified as a center of LGBTQ—or "gay," as the press referred to it then—life in Chicago. It also had a recent history of supporting candidates who were independent of Chicago's infamous Democratic political machine.

Interestingly, though there had been a continuous history of organized LGBTQ activism in Chicago at least since the mid-1960s, Nepon was completely unknown among movement participants. As he admitted to the press in the first round of interviews after he announced his candidacy in October, "I am not a gay activist." But the successful and highly publicized campaign of Anita Bryant earlier in 1977 to repeal the gay rights law in Dade County "hit me like a brick," according to his Statement of Candidacy. It provoked him to attend his first LGBTQ demonstration, despite being, in his words, "a businessman with a name to protect." But Nepon felt he could no longer remain silent about gay issues, and so, a few months after that first demonstration, he decided to run for public office. He made clear that he was not a "single-issue" candidate. He stood for full access to abortion, including state funding for low-income women; no-fault divorce law; increased funding of public schools; and an expansion of state-supported children and family services. He supported ratification by Illinois of the Equal Rights Amendment. And he was also choosing to wear his identity as a gay man openly and proudly, even if he was not emphasizing LGBTQ issues in the campaign.

One might assume that the queer community in Chicago would have jumped at the chance to rally behind one of its own. But nothing could be further from the truth. Nepon received virtually no endorsements of consequence from anyone in the community. Chuck Renslow, a gay entrepreneur and activist who was a precinct captain on the North Side, did not support him. *Gay Life*, the main community newspaper, did not endorse him. In the view of Grant Ford, its publisher and editor, "the incumbents are our friends." Nepon was running against incumbents (at this time, Illinois had state legislative districts that elected multiple candidates to the assembly) who had already shown their support for the community, according to

Ford. Nepon was wrong in assuming, as Renslow expressed it, that "the community will vote for him just because he's gay."

Nepon's inexperience in the world of politics showed in his campaign. One reporter described him as "shy and unpolished." He had to be "coaxed into working the streets." At one point in the campaign, much of his staff resigned in frustration. When the votes were counted, Ford and Renslow were proven right. Nepon placed a distant last among the four candidates, and, after the primary, he simply disappeared and was never heard from again in the world of Chicago LGBTQ activism.

So, what should we make of all this? Was his candidacy of no consequence? Was it nothing but a quirky oddity, a momentary distraction from the growing movement activism of the 1970s? The historical evidence suggests otherwise.

What the campaign unquestionably produced was a level of press attention in Chicago that the LGBTQ movement did not yet commonly receive. The mainstream press seemed fascinated by Chicago's "first avowed gay candidate," as more than one newspaper described him. When San Francisco's Harvey Milk, perhaps *the* gay political celebrity of the era, came to Chicago in a show of support for Nepon, it provided another excuse for journalists to report on what was otherwise a lackluster campaign. The *Chicago Reader*, a politically progressive weekly that was widely read, started their article about him, which ran for several pages, on its front cover. The headline read "Is Nepon the Great Gay Hope of Chicago?" The *Reader* reported that Nepon's campaign was raising the specter of "Gay Clout" at the ballot box and thereby pushing other Chicago politicians to pay attention to this newly mobilized community.

As it turned out, Nepon was not the Great Gay Hope. But the *Reader* closed with a comment that does capture one way in which this was an important moment. "If the Nepon candidacy accomplishes nothing else, it has, for the movement at least, produced a new political phenomenon in Chicago: political candidates battling with each other to be the biggest friend of the gay community." Sometimes, even a personal defeat can be a movement victory.

16

Ten Years after Stonewall: The Police Are Still Attacking Us

Across the United States, and especially in Chicago, police behavior in recent years has been a major news thread. The unjustifiable killing of African American males, the rise of the Black Lives Matter movement, the exposure of systematic police brutality that forces confessions from arrestees who had committed no crime, the resistance of urban police departments to investigating and disciplining their officers: all this and more have put police under scrutiny.

Historically, urban police departments have played a key role in the oppression of LGBTQ people. Police commonly raided gay and lesbian bars and arrested both employees and patrons. Plainclothes officers entrapped gay and bisexual men in parks and on the streets and charged them with sexual solicitation. Transgender individuals and other gender nonconformists found themselves arrested for the violation of laws that prohibited what was described as "cross-dressing." Disorderly conduct, lewd behavior, public indecency: the police had a range of charges readily at their disposal. Is it any wonder that the gay liberation era was ushered in by the police raid of a gay bar in New York City's Greenwich Village? The uprising at the Stonewall Inn in June 1969 provides powerful commentary on how central aggressive police behavior has been in the construction

The research for this essay is based on the David Boyer Papers, Gerber/Hart Library and Archives.

of LGBTQ oppression as well as in the building of a movement to fight it.

As is widely recognized, the resistance to the bar raid and the arrests at the Stonewall quickly launched a whole new phase of the LGBTQ fight against oppression. As earlier essays in this collection have discussed, organizations like Chicago Gay Liberation, the Chicago Gay Alliance, and the Transvestite Legal Committee formed in Chicago soon after. In the course of the 1970s, the number of LGBTQ organizations in the United States rose from a few dozen to more than a thousand. Important victories were achieved. The American Psychiatric Association eliminated homosexuality from its list of mental illnesses. The federal government dropped its blanket ban on the employment of gay, lesbian, and bisexual individuals. Several states repealed their sodomy laws. Debates opened up in a wide range of communities of faith that had previously seen homosexual acts and relationships as immoral. The first cities and towns began passing ordinances that prohibited discrimination based on sexual orientation. A few men and women who had openly acknowledged that they were gay or lesbian were elected to public office. And, above all, more individuals came out as gay, lesbian, bisexual, or transgender.

What was the response of law enforcement to these upheavals? How did urban police react to the changes that were starting to occur in the 1970s? The papers of David Boyer offer a revealing look into police behavior in Chicago a decade after the Stonewall Rebellion and the birth of gay liberation. Boyer was the manager of Carol's Speakeasy, a popular gay bar in the Old Town neighborhood of Chicago. He was also involved with the Gay and Lesbian Coalition of Metropolitan Chicago, an effort in the late 1970s to put the wide range of activist groups and LGBTQ businesses in dialogue with each other.

The spring of 1979 saw disturbing developments in Chicago, just weeks before the tenth anniversary of Stonewall and the birth of gay liberation. At this time, the Halsted Street corridor in Lakeview had not yet morphed into "Boystown." The Near North and Old Town neighborhoods were still key centers of LGBTQ nightlife, with several bars as well as park spaces that were cruising grounds for gay and bisexual men and transwomen. As winter was ending and bar patrons on weekend nights often spilled onto the streets, heterosexual residents who were hostile to the queer presence phoned in complaints to the police. Police readily used the calls as their justification for entering the bars, sometimes in plainclothes, to observe patrons and then make arrests. Howard Goodman, the co-owner of New Flight, a Near North bar on Clark Street, told a *Chicago Sun-Times* reporter that, in the space of three months, the police had "come in here 27 times . . . to search people for no reason, and they won't answer when you ask them why they're doing it." Another bar owner, who was not identified by the reporter, said that "the police are cracking down on gay bars all over the North Side."

Anger about the harassment first broke into the open at a May 10 public meeting of Chicago's Police Board. Joe Murray, who worked as a liaison to the LGBTQ community for State Assembly Representative Jesse White, grilled Superintendent James O'Grady about police behavior. Murray told O'Grady that nine bars had been raided recently. Raising the specter of the police department's well-known loyalty to Chicago's political machine, he asked if O'Grady had ordered the raids as retaliation because of the community's support for Mayor Jane Byrne. O'Grady naturally denied the accusation and claimed not to know about the raids at all. After Murray described the police as using "storm trooper tactics," Joseph McCarthy, who was the commander of the police district that was conducting the raids, shouted "This is a lot of bullshit" and left abruptly.

Just ten days later, police attacks escalated. On the night of Saturday, May 19, police raided New Flight yet again, arresting the managers for "keeping a disorderly house" and a patron for "public indecency." After midnight, plainclothes officers began infiltrating the crowd at Carol's Speakeasy, perhaps the city's most popular gay bar. At a certain point, they announced themselves and ordered the evacuation of the bar, whose patrons numbered almost six hundred.

Uniformed police were outside on Wells Street in droves and began dispersing the crowd. When someone with a camera started taking pictures, police assaulted him, smashed the camera, seized the film, and left the photographer with injuries that required having his arm in a sling. Another arrestee received injuries serious enough to place him in an intensive care unit. Altogether, eleven men were placed under arrest. When a few activists convened on the district police station, the desk sergeant subjected them to verbal abuse. "Mind your own business," he told them, "or I'll stick you in lock up with the rest of the assholes, and you can all suck each other's dicks."

The raid at Carol's Speakeasy was of such a size that the city's newspapers reported on it. But the nature of the coverage suggests how uncomfortable the mainstream media still was at the end of the 1970s when dealing with LGBTQ issues. The *Sun-Times*, for instance, described New Flight as "a reputed gay bar." The *Tribune* characterized Carol's as having "a reputation as a gathering place for homosexuals." The papers also gave considerable space to the police version of events, reporting on underage drinking, illegal sexual activity, and public indecency. "We act on citizens' complaints," one police sergeant told a reporter. The *Sun-Times* attributed the arrests to a fight that erupted outside the bar, while the *Tribune* classified the situation as a "melee" that required the police to seize the participants.

The community response was immediate. Word went out quickly that an open meeting would be held on Monday night, less than forty-eight hours after the raid at Carol's. Over five hundred people showed up. They decided to hold a march and rally two weeks later, on June 5. An ad hoc group formed to plan and coordinate. A letter was sent to Mayor Jane Byrne accusing the police of "insulting language, verbal threats . . . and physical brutality to the point of hospitalization" and calling on Byrne to show solidarity by appearing at the rally. Flyers were distributed in bars, and bar owners were asked to close between six and ten o'clock that night to encourage a larger turnout. Chants reflected the spirit of the participants, which was both militant and, as so often surfaces in queer activism, humorous.

"We are Gay! We are Proud! We are Peaceful! We are Loud!" was one. And to the tune of "Frère Jacques," marchers sang:

Superintendent, Superintendent
What's the score? What's the score?
We won't take harassment, we won't take harassment
Anymore, anymore!

Meanwhile, during these months, Boyer had been representing Carol's Speakeasy at meetings of the Gay and Lesbian Coalition of Metropolitan Chicago. Formed in 1975, it was intended to bring together, for the purpose of united responses, both activist organizations and businesses catering to the community. Shockingly, the coalition was surprisingly unresponsive toward the police raids. In April, at a point when the wave of police appearances at bars had already begun, the coalition actually disbanded its Committee to Investigate Police Harassment of Gay Bars. After the massive community meeting in response to the major raid, the coalition's minutes noted its occurrence but lacked any mention of a decision to act. By June, in the wake of the large march and rally, the coalition held an open community forum in which dissatisfaction with the coalition was undisguised. Expressing their displeasure with its passivity in the face of events, attendees urged it to be "more activist-oriented, more focused, and more politically oriented." As someone said to the room as a whole, "we need to bring the Coalition back to life."

Reading about these conflicts with the police in Chicago as the tenth anniversary of the Stonewall Uprising approached, I found myself reflecting upon the fact that Chicago's situation was not unique. On May 21, just two nights after the massive raid of Carol's Speakeasy and the same night that hundreds were gathering in a community meeting to plan a response, LGBTQ San Franciscans were marching to City Hall from the Castro neighborhood to protest the light sentence that Dan White received for the killing of Harvey Milk, San Francisco's gay city supervisor, and Mayor George Moscone. The police response was immediate. Masses of officers descended upon the Castro, invading gay bars and beating individuals on the street. In both San Francisco and Chicago, and no doubt in other cities as well, queer people were still seen by the police as easy and deserving targets of abuse.

As it turned out, the timing of the police raids in Chicago—as well as the so-called White Night Riots in San Francisco—encouraged a much larger turnout for the tenth anniversary Pride Marches at the end of June than had ever been seen before. Bar raids in Chicago did not immediately end, but in the course of the 1980s, they did become noticeably less frequent. During the mayoral years of Harold Washington (1983–87), a progressive African American who was not part of the Chicago political machine, raids finally stopped. Only a sustained, vocal community response had the power to make that happen.

17

Trying to Work Together: The Gay and Lesbian Coalition of Metropolitan Chicago

A key source of excitement in studying movements for social justice comes from the uncovering of past victories and forgotten heroes in the struggle of a community against oppression. Writing history can be a way to inspire and motivate activism in the present by restoring to memory a proud heritage of resistance. But history is also more complex than that. It contains stories of failures and frustrations as well.

The history of the Gay and Lesbian Coalition of Metropolitan Chicago, which surfaced in the account of the bar raids of 1979, brings this complexity to light. The coalition formed in 1975, at a point when the radicalism and militancy associated with the first wave of gay liberation and lesbian feminism had faded considerably. A diversity of activists, ranging from Chuck Renslow, the owner of several sex businesses and very much a machine-politics type, to Bill Kelley, an activist in the liberal reform tradition, to Christine Riddiough, a democratic socialist feminist, joined forces to create a mechanism to mobilize community members more easily. They cast a very wide net in their outreach efforts, as they invited into the coalition not only explicitly activist organizations but also businesses serving the community.

The research for this essay is based on the records of the Gay and Lesbian Coalition of Metropolitan Chicago, Gerber/Hart Library and Archives.

The minutes of coalition meetings reveal the ways that sustaining the coalition was an uphill struggle. Even in 1977, when the campaign of beauty queen and popular singer Anita Bryant to repeal a gay rights law in Dade County, Florida, was rousing LGBTQ people across America, the coalition had a hard time persuading groups and businesses to join. LGBTQ organizations in these years were almost all dependent on volunteers; participating in the coalition simply added to the workload of activists often on the edge of burnout. Businesses in the community were also stretched thin and unable to spare the time to get involved; many did not want to be associated with political causes or antagonize the police. Thus, despite the fact that the coalition's minutes in October 1977 reported reaching out to thirty-seven organizations and businesses, few were choosing to participate. This failure seemed to create a vicious circle, as the underresourced coalition came to seem "slow moving" in the eyes of many and therefore not worth their time and energy.

Whatever the coalition's undeniable limitations, its history still offers revealing insights into the range of issues that motivated LGBTQ activists in Chicago in the second half of the 1970s. Even after the repeal of the Dade County law prohibiting discrimination based on sexual orientation, the specter of Anita Bryant continued to spark activist responses. The coalition promoted a boycott of Florida citrus products, especially Tropicana juices, since Bryant was the celebrity face in many of the industry's ads. After Bryant's appearance in June 1977 at the Medinah Temple in Chicago provoked a massive demonstration that included arrests, the coalition provided court observers to make sure the defendants were treated fairly. The coalition committed funds to support the travel of Chicago-area lesbians to the International Women's Year Conference held in Houston in 1977, perhaps the major event in the US feminist movement that year. It provided financial assistance to lesbian mothers forced to fight in court to retain custody of their children born through a heterosexual marriage. It publicly condemned the discriminatory treatment that LGBTQ inmates received at the hands of Chicago's correctional system, such as the denial of access to publications like the community newspaper, *Gay Life*. It debated whether Chicago's Pride Parade, held in June with an array of floats, should be reconceptualized as a march against discrimination and oppression. And it conducted a "Racism and Sexism Survey" to assess the state of relations within the LGBTQ community and evaluate what kind of internal community issues might need attention.

The work of the coalition also illuminates events beyond Chicago. Although the LGBTQ movement in the 1970s consisted overwhelmingly of local activist groups, some national organizations were beginning to form. There were definitely efforts to build support for coordinated actions and to share movement-building skills. In July 1977, the coalition sent Chris Riddiough and Bill Kelley to a National Gay Conference held in Denver. The conference, which brought together about three hundred activists from across the United States, was jointly sponsored by four organizations: Troy Perry's Metropolitan Community Church network; Dignity, the organization of LGBTQ Catholics that was growing rapidly at this time; and the National Gay Task Force and the Gay Rights National Lobby, both of which were in the early stages of working to influence policy at the federal level.

The panel presentations and plenary speeches provide a good sense of what was claiming the attention of activists that year. High on the list, naturally, was Anita Bryant and the Dade County defeat, which brought sustained media attention to gay and lesbian issues for the first time. But there was also extended discussion about the prospects for progress at the national level. A sexual orientation antidiscrimination bill had been introduced in Congress for the first time in 1974, and the administration of Jimmy Carter, who became president at the start of 1977, was showing a surprising receptivity to engage in dialogue with community representatives. Other key topics included discussions of strategy and tactics for state and local lobbying; how to improve media coverage of gay and lesbian issues; and the importance of organizing in religious communities. Attendees at the conference also passed resolutions endorsing the Equal Rights Amendment, supporting International Women's Year, calling for the boycott of Florida citrus products and of Coors beer, and declaring respect for gay and lesbian youth. The brief report on the conference, written by Riddiough and Kelley, whetted my curiosity to learn more about the event—the planning that went into it, what organizations and individuals participated, and the impact afterward, especially in terms of strengthening activist networks across the United States and engaging in future coordinated activities.

Digging through the papers of the coalition brought unexpected reminders of dramatic differences between the past and the present. Already by the mid-1970s, the movement in Illinois was pushing for legislative recognition. Bills to prohibit discrimination based on sexual orientation had been introduced into the state legislature in Springfield. Hearings were held before the House Judiciary Committee in April 1977 on a bill affecting some forms of Illinois state employment, and a debate occurred on the house floor in May. But, in 1977, legislation like this was still beyond the pale for most elected officials, and the bill suffered a massive defeat in the house—a mere thirty-eight in favor and 114 against.

Most surprisingly, however, the two sponsors who led the fight for the legislation were Susan Catania and Elroy Sundquist—and both of them were Republicans! In an era in which Republicans are the party of Donald Trump, Mitch McConnell, Mike Pence, and Ted Cruz, it has become hard even to imagine that Republicans were ever strong proponents of gay and lesbian equality. But in the 1970s, Republicans and Democrats could each still be considered "coalition" parties. Each consisted of conservatives, moderates, and liberals. Admittedly, that was in the process of change. Many traditionally Democratic white southerners were shifting to the Republicans in the wake of civil rights legislation pushed by the national Democratic Party. And white Christian evangelicals were also embracing the Republican Party as a response to the rise of both feminism and gay liberation and the association of liberal Democrats with these new movements. By the 1980s, with the Reagan presidency and the growing number of Republicans in Congress, this would begin to shift more dramatically, and the polarization that characterizes twenty-first-century party politics was underway. But, in the mid-1970s, at least in Illinois, Republicans could emerge as leading supporters of LGBTQ rights.

18

Knowledge Is Power: Chicago's Gay Academic Union

At the University of Illinois at Chicago, where I taught for fifteen years, there is a Gender and Sexuality Center that provides services, meeting places, and programming for queer students. There is a Chancellor's Committee on LGBTQ Concerns, which receives funding, has access to upper-level administrators, and makes recommendations about changes in campus policies. There are many "out" faculty who do research on LGBTQ topics. There is a Gender and Women's Studies Program with courses related to LGBTQ history, culture, and experience. And the school year ends with an annual Lavender Graduation, which is a joyous celebration of student success. UIC admittedly has a reputation as an especially LGBTQ-friendly campus. But its situation is not unique. LGBTQ people, issues, and research are very visible on college and university campuses across the United States.

Needless to say, this has not always been the case. A full history of how scholarly research, writing, and teaching developed and how a visible LGBTQ presence became institutionalized in US higher education has not yet been written. But when that does finally happen, an important early piece of the history will be the story of the Gay Academic Union and the work it did in the 1970s and 1980s.

I was part of the small but steadily growing group that began

The research for this essay is based on the Randy Grisham Papers, the Stan Huntington Papers, and the James Manahan Papers, all in the Gerber/Hart Library and Archives.

meeting in New York early in 1973 and eventually formed the GAU. It served an invaluable networking and support function at a time when undergraduates were taking the lead in coming out, while most university faculty, graduate students, and staff were still in the closet and very little nonhomophobic research was being done. I helped plan the first three national conferences, held in New York over Thanksgiving weekend in 1973, 1974, and 1975. Roughly three hundred people came to the first; by 1975, almost a thousand attended. (The proceedings of that first conference, and an account of how the GAU was formed, can be found on the website of Outhistory.org.)

For several years, Chicago had a GAU chapter. Three of its members—Randy Grisham, Stan Huntington, and James Manahan—all donated papers to Gerber/Hart. They provide insight into the local workings of the organization as well as its national structure and activities. Reading through them, and especially the Grisham collection, which has the most material, I came away with a clearer picture of both the extent of the national network that GAU sustained and the local workings of the Chicago chapter.

Above all, in the context of the 1970s, when most LGBTQ individuals were not open about their identities, the national Gay Academic Union allowed local chapters to feel they were part of a bigger network. A list of GAU chapters in 1979 included not just obvious places, like New York, San Francisco, and Los Angeles, but also cities like Saint Louis, Dallas, and Greensboro, North Carolina. The national GAU, which by the end of the 1970s was based in Los Angeles, maintained a mailing list of six thousand, quite impressive for those times. It held national conferences that drew hundreds and allowed attendees to connect with people beyond their own city of residence.

The Chicago chapter formed in 1978. It held its first conference the following year, in May 1979. Only fifty people attended. But when it organized a second conference in 1980, attendance jumped to 250. And in 1982, when it hosted the organization's national conference, over four hundred came to it, and there were more than sixty sessions. The conferences, as well as public lectures that it sponsored, allowed GAU to bring some of the authors of the first books on LGBTQ history, culture, and politics to Chicago. Speakers included academic scholars like James Steakley, who did pioneering research on the early gay movement in Germany and whose work initially appeared in the *Body Politic*, a radical gay liberation paper published in Toronto; Lillian Faderman, whose *Surpassing the Love of Men* covered several hundred years of women's intimate relationships with each other and who has since become a prolific author of books on queer history; and John Boswell, whose *Christianity, Social Tolerance, and Homosexuality* was a publishing sensation when it appeared in 1980. Community-based scholars were also represented. Vito Russo, the author of *The Celluloid Closet*, presented on how Hollywood's films from the silent era through the 1970s had portrayed LGBTQ characters and themes, while Allan Bérubé, who was researching the history of gay men and lesbians during World War II, delivered his lecture "Marching to a Different Drummer." Conferences such as these gave visibility to the intellectual and cultural work being done. They also created connections among researchers nationwide as well as helped to build community locally.

Besides functioning as something of a network node, GAU in Chicago also served as incubator for other projects. One of its members, Gregory Sprague, who was a graduate student in history at the University of Chicago, used GAU as a base from which to launch a Chicago Gay and Lesbian History Project. Among its features was a Chicago-based oral history project that he initiated and that conducted some of the interviews discussed in earlier chapters in this collection. Sprague went on to do extensive research on Chicago's pre-Stonewall LGBTQ history, going back to the early twentieth century. He put together an illustrated slide lecture, "The Making of the Modern Homosexual" (this was before the days of PowerPoint presentations), that he not only gave many times to audiences in Chicago, but that he also presented around the country. Sprague was also a key player in helping to organize historians within the American Historical Association.

Another project that GAU in Chicago helped launch was a community-based library. It began collecting a wide range of books, both fiction and nonfiction, on LGBTQ topics. Such books were far less common than they are today, and individuals accessed books almost entirely by either borrowing them from a library or buying them in a bookstore. To check a book out or purchase one felt like an act of coming out to the many who were still in the closet. Thus, a library created and run by the community was a particularly valuable resource in these years. By November 1981, when the library opened as an independent organization at 3245 Sheffield Road, it was named the Gerber/Hart Library and had a collection of over a thousand LGBTQ-related books, an extraordinarily large number for those times. Since then, it has grown into a major community-based history archive.

By the late 1970s, GAU was facing increasing difficulties as a national organization. In 1985 the national office closed, taking many of its local chapters down with it. There appeared to be tension, as often happens in movement organizations, between the national headquarters and local chapters. One letter to the national office from 1979 charged that "GAU is being run . . . by a clique in Los Angeles that does not want any input." But GAU also seemed to be undone by its own successes. As GAU created a safe environment for LGBTQ faculty in higher education to meet and discuss issues, it made it more likely that these individuals would begin networking and organizing within their own professional associations—among other historians, anthropologists, sociologists, psychologists, literary scholars, and members of other academic disciplines as well. This gradual shift toward an "out" world within the academy also highlights the challenge that a local chapter like Chicago's faced. Most of its members and most of those who attended its events were not academic faculty. But as faculty faded from the scene, their audiences in effect had nothing to draw them together.

As a closing note, one of the great pleasures of doing archival research comes from an unexpected discovery—not so much something that profoundly changes my interpretation of the past, but rather adds a vivid, humorous, or surprising detail. Exploring the papers of Randy Grisham provided such a moment. At the national Gay Academic Union conference in 1982 that the Chicago chapter hosted at the Conrad Hilton Hotel, Randy Shilts was one of the plenary session speakers. Shilts was already perhaps the highest-profile openly gay journalist in the United States. His biography of Harvey Milk, *The Mayor of Castro Street*, had just come out, and a few years later he would publish *And the Band Played On*, an account of the early years of the AIDS epidemic that garnered national media attention. Shilts was described as delivering a "rambling" address, during which he happened to mention casually that he had just smoked marijuana.

19

Sexual Orientation and the Law

Focusing upon Chicago's LGBTQ history is a form of what is often described as "local" history, writing about a particular place within a larger nation. Yet, local history also extends beyond the place it describes. The local can be used to illustrate broader historical patterns and to make generalizations about an era or a topic. And, sometimes, a place like Chicago can be the setting for events that might be considered national in their reach and consequence.

Such was the case in April 1987 when Chicago hosted the conference "Sexual Orientation and the Law." Held at the University of Chicago, it was put together by the Gay and Lesbian Law Students Association at the university. Irwin Keller, who was a student at the law school, was one of the core organizers. His papers provide great insight into the state of the law in the mid-1980s and the strategic thinking of key legal activists.

The conference came at a critical moment. By 1987, we were several years into the AIDS epidemic, with caseloads and deaths growing in number exponentially. The Reagan presidency was unrelentingly hostile to anything gay, completely ignored the AIDS crisis, and welcomed the religious right into the center of the Republican Party. And, as all this was going on, in June 1986 a five-to-four Supreme Court decision in the *Bowers v. Hardwick* case upheld the con-

The research for this essay is based on the Irwin Keller Papers, Gerber/Hart Library and Archives.

stitutionality of state sodomy laws. Bad as the decision was in itself, the language used by the justices in the majority was overtly hostile and derogatory. It described the claims made by those challenging the constitutionality of sodomy statutes as "facetious." The laws, it said, were rooted in "millennia of moral teaching." The Constitution offered "no such thing as a fundamental right to commit homosexual sodomy."

But sometimes defeats can have benefits. *Hardwick* was a spur to action. It helped create the demand for a national March on Washington, scheduled for October 1987, a march that, as a later essay will describe, proved to be a demonstration of staggeringly large numbers. And it provided the impetus for members of the Gay and Lesbian Law Students Association at the University of Chicago to propose and organize the first national conference on sexual orientation and the law, scheduled for April 11, 1987.

Organizers of the conference cast a wide net. They sent mailings announcing the conference to every law school in the country, hoping not only to reach law students everywhere but also, perhaps, to spur LGBTQ law students to organize. Estimates of the number who attended the conference that day ranged from five to six hundred. The conference planners also sent invitations to participate to a broad range of legal activists and constitutional lawyers.

The list of those who spoke at the conference reads like a roll call of the pioneers in queer legal activism: Thomas Stoddard, executive director of Lambda Legal Defense, the first national gay and lesbian legal organization; Abby Rubenfeld, who was Lambda's legal director; Nan Hunter, the founding director of the ACLU's Lesbian and Gay Rights Project; Roberta Achtenberg, the chief attorney for the National Lesbian Rights Project; and Nancy Polikoff, who had been an attorney for the Women's Legal Defense Fund and helped cut a path for feminist and LGBTQ family law. Another attendee, Mary Dunlap, just a few weeks before had argued the "Gay Olympics" case before the Supreme Court and was awaiting the Court's decision in the case.

At times the tone of the sessions was somber. On the opening panel, Tom Stoddard commented on the impact of *Hardwick*. Looking back on some earlier lower court victories, he said that *Hardwick* "erases that progress in the federal courts to a very strong degree and also creates a climate in the courts that makes it harder to win on state issues as well." Evaluating the state of immigration law as it related to lesbians and gays, another panelist frankly said "it is a mess . . . [it] is not only confusing, it's ridiculous." Panelists debated whether it made more sense in the future to argue cases on the basis of equal protection principles or from the perspective of the right to privacy. Equal protection would effectively create for sexual orientation the same level of legal rights that accrued to race and gender. Were the courts—and the nation—ready for that? Privacy, on the other hand, would rely on a core constitutional principle of individual rights and personal liberty.

A theme that surfaced repeatedly was the impact that the AIDS epidemic was having. It was stoking deeply irrational prejudice in American society toward gay and bisexual men especially. David Schulman, a lawyer who handled AIDS-related cases in Los Angeles, described the atmosphere as permeated by "primal fears." AIDS was encouraging more overt discrimination and then justifying that discrimination because of the threat posed to public health.

Yet there was also a fighting tone to many of the presentations and discussions. Despite the outcome in *Hardwick*, speakers agreed that it was "a risk we had to take." The loss in the Supreme Court would hopefully encourage activists to work for state repeal, thus building activism and political consciousness locally while also pushing lawyers to explore whether some state constitutions might provide grounds for court challenges. Panelists identified some areas of law as sites of important victories. Stoddard described the area of public employment as the place where "lodestar" cases had brought "significant victory." Discussions of family law seemed to produce the highest level of energy. In 1987, no state gave legal recognition to same-sex intimate relationships, and state cases about child custody for lesbian mothers were mixed in their outcome. Anticipating the intensifying focus that the 1990s and beyond would bring to marriage and other forms of family law, Abby Rubenfeld stated unambiguously that "we need the sanction of the state," and Nan Hunter declared "we should have it all." Hunter explained her support of a fight for access to marriage in terms of "the power of marriage as a symbol." Taking a broad view beyond the *Hardwick* defeat and the challenges created by AIDS, Rubenfeld reminded her audience that, in comparison to conditions twenty years earlier, "tremendous legal progress has been made." She encouraged her legal colleagues to keep fighting. In choosing cases, she argued, activist lawyers had to "balance realism and practicality with foresight and vision."

Most of all, perhaps, the conference was valuable because of the power of bringing so many legal activists together to form and strengthen working relationships and to discuss what the future might bring. As Keller described it in a letter he wrote years later, "it was a hugely exciting event—the air was alive with crisis and possibility." And, for Keller and the other students who had helped organize the conference, there was a local dimension to their excitement. Just days before the event, the University of Chicago had witnessed a dramatic display of homophobia. A group on campus calling itself the "Great White Brotherhood of the Iron Fist" had claimed responsibility for what Keller described as "a spate of horrible homophobic attacks against students and community members." Five hundred people attending a national conference called "Sexual Orientation and the Law" served as a powerful response to the homophobia of these extremists and a reminder that the fight for freedom, equality, and acceptance was vitally necessary.

20

A Lesbian Community Center in Chicago

As a "gay world" became increasingly visible in the course of the 1970s, to most of the heterosexual majority it must have seemed like one unified mass. But, as several previous essays suggest, unity was not a characteristic that commonly described either LGBTQ activists or the larger community. There were divisions based on the different life experiences that came because of an individual's multiple identities—identities and experiences such as those based on race, ethnicity, gender, class, and religious affiliation, among others. There were deep divisions as well based on one's approaches to activism and movement building—a multi-issue coalition-style politics or a solitary focus on gay rights; a militant, disruptive activism or a commitment to working by the existing rules of politics and other institutions. The splits that occurred in Chicago Gay Liberation, the unwillingness of many activists to support Gary Nepon, the difficulty that the Gay and Lesbian Coalition of Metropolitan Chicago faced in reaching a united approach even to something as outrageous as police raids on bars: all highlight the immense challenges of having all segments of the LGBTQ community join forces and create a united movement.

In the 1970s and 1980s, these internal divisions most frequently displayed themselves between gay men and lesbians. Many of the

The research for this essay is based on the records of the Lesbian Community Center, Gerber/Hart Library and Archives.

lesbians who were politicized around their sexual identity came to the movement with a strong feminist consciousness. The unaware ingrained sexism of many gay men, their failure to see that the key issues facing men and women were often not the same, and their inability to allow space—both literally and figuratively—for the needs of lesbians, led many women to go off on their own to build organizations that spoke to their specific needs. The drive to create and sustain lesbian-centered space and projects was a key form of activism in these decades.

* * *

"Community centers" have become a staple of LGBTQ life in major cities in the twenty-first century. Today, they typically have paid staff and a large board of directors. They often have a significant donor base and receive government funds and foundation grants. They provide a range of services to youth, elders, and other groups within the LGBTQ population. The centers serve as a dependable meeting place for other community organizations, and they are a site for major community events. They may be located in buildings with a large array of offices and meeting spaces. They may have budgets in the millions of dollars, and they are likely to be open during the day and the evening and during the week and on weekends. In Chicago currently, the Center on Halsted very much displays these characteristics.

Needless to say, this wasn't always so. Chicago's earliest community center, created by the Chicago Gay Alliance in 1971, occupied rental space in a house. The organization brought a lot of enthusiasm to the project, but with few financial resources and depending entirely on volunteer labor, the center barely lasted a handful of years before it had to close its doors.

Most of these early efforts at establishing community centers were dominated by white men, not only numerically, but also in the kind of activities and interests that the centers supported. In many cities, open conflict developed over the efforts of lesbians to have the space be welcoming to them as well. Los Angeles was one of the cities where, in the 1970s, these tensions erupted into bitterly fought public battles.

In some cities, lesbians attempted to form their own community centers. But the challenges for lesbians in the 1970s and early 1980s were even greater than those faced by the efforts led by gay men. The deeply structural gender bias in employment and wages made it harder for women who were attracted to women to live as lesbians. Those who were out were likely to have fewer economic resources to sustain a community center. And, in this era, many lesbians had a primary commitment to a broader feminist activism.

A lesbian community center did open in Chicago at the end of 1978. After a few months of sharing space with another feminist organization, it moved to a rental space of two rooms in a building near Wrigley Field in the Lakeview neighborhood. It maintained evening hours during the week and afternoon hours on Saturday and Sunday, a significant achievement. The center accumulated a lending library at a time when LGBTQ books were not so easily available. Describing itself as "a referral-information service and drop-in space," it explicitly defined itself as "an alternative to the bars for all women."

A monthly newsletter described the broad range of services and activities that the center offered. There were support groups for black women, large women, women over thirty-five, and women under twenty-one. There were picnics in warmer weather, potluck dinners, bridge nights, and game nights. The center put together its own softball team, which played against other women's teams in Chicago. It brought in speakers to give educational talks, such as the local community historian Marie Kuda, who presented slide lectures on the history of lesbian literature. Music nights were a common event, with a number of local women musicians and singers performing.

A major goal of the center was to create solidarity and networks of support among and between lesbians and the many women-centered initiatives that were sprouting up in these years. Its bulletin board was packed with notices about upcoming events of other organizations, services provided by other women, and the search for roommates and living spaces. To help meet its expenses, the center made a point of selling merchandise made by women. It sold books published by Metis Press, a Chicago-based women's publishing firm. It offered posters, T-shirts, candles, menstrual sponges, and many other items, all created by women artists and entrepreneurs.

And, of course, the center promoted political mobilization. In March 1980, the state legislature had scheduled public hearings in Chicago for a proposed state law prohibiting discrimination based on sexual orientation. The center urged all its members and visitors to show up at the hearing so that the room would be packed. That spring, it put together a contingent that participated in a major "Support the Equal Rights Amendment" march. The contingent was large enough to be mentioned in the *Chicago Sun-Times* coverage of the event. And it had a contingent in the Pride Parade in June.

The materials in this particular archival collection are not expansive enough to be able to reconstruct a full and detailed history of the organization. But, for someone wanting to put together a history of lesbian life in Chicago in this era in its social, cultural, and political dimensions, there is much that is revealing. For instance, a binder marked "Resources, A to Z," and dated January 1, 1982, contains the names of individual organizations as well as organizations grouped by categories. Arranged alphabetically from "Bars" to "Third World Women's Resources," the list included such categories as Collectives/Coops, Ecumenical Organizations, Music, Political Organizations, Publications, Radio Programs, Suburban Rap Groups, and many others. The scope of the list is very suggestive of the breadth of independent lesbian organizing in these years.

There are also three boxes of three-by-five index cards. One is a "Library Users File" with names and addresses. Another has the names of volunteers, what they are able to offer the center, and when they are available. Yet another file related to volunteers included an activity log for a stretch of time in 1982 and 1983. And there is a "Library Circulation File" in which each card lists a book and its author and who has borrowed the book. These various files of names often include zip codes and street addresses. As I flipped through all these cards, I could readily imagine a determined researcher using these to construct a list of addresses designed to identify residential areas where lesbians were concentrated. The volunteer logs allow for the reconstruction of the kind of services provided by the center and the activities that most engaged lesbian patrons. The library circulation records would provide insight into the books that were most popular among lesbians in this period. Profiles of activists might also emerge in the course of this close examination.

The trail of documents in this collection ends in 1983. There is no indication whether the center closed at that time. As we will see in a later essay, a renewed effort to open a lesbian community center surfaced again at the end of the decade, so it is clear that this version of a center had a limited life span. But, even though it closed, other initiatives in Chicago were bringing lesbians together and creating a visible lesbian culture.

21

The Artemis Singers and the Power of Music

As someone who is not particularly musical, thinking about the place of music and performance in history poses challenges. Music certainly has played an important role at various moments in the past. No one would dispute, for instance, the importance of music in the civil rights movement or in white youth culture and protest in the 1960s. But how does one evaluate its impact? How does it fit into the chronicle of a movement? How does it foster change in other spheres of society?

For anyone interested in music and the place it deserves in writing history, the story of the Artemis Singers could easily serve as a case study. Artemis was a self-consciously lesbian chorus. It saw itself as "an educational political vehicle for changing negative stereotypes about lesbians." When it formed in the summer of 1980, a world of women's music was growing rapidly. Women's music festivals were sprouting up around the country, and there were at least a couple of dozen all-women and openly feminist choral groups. Yet, as Susan Schleef, the founding director of Artemis, noted, among these groups in the early 1980s there was only one other self-declared lesbian chorus. Schleef and the members of Artemis had as one of their core goals "to increase our visibility in the feminist commu-

The research for this essay is based on the records of the Artemis Singers, Gerber/Hart Library and Archives.

nity," especially because music events across the United States were becoming public spaces of feminist solidarity.

Artemis jumped right into this world. It joined the Sister Singers Network, which was founded at a meeting in Saint Louis in 1980 and by 1981 already had twenty-five choruses as members. Sister Singers Network kept these choruses in communication with each other and coordinated the planning of major events. Schleef and other Artemis members participated in the first Midwest Women's Music Festival, held in the Ozarks in 1982, and they helped make it into an annual event in the 1980s.

Besides its work in the thriving milieu of women's music, Artemis also thrust itself into the newly emerging world of gay choral performance. In Chicago in 1979, two musical groups had formed, the Windy City Gay Chorus and the Chicago Gay and Lesbian Community Band, and they were beginning to perform at major events like the annual Pride March and Festival. An umbrella group, Toddlin' Town Performing Arts, was created to provide nonprofit status and allow money to be raised to support the groups. Artemis became the third member of Toddlin' Town and provided a lesbian presence at its meetings, where performances and other events were planned. At the time Artemis joined, the board of directors was entirely male, and there was, in the words of one Artemis member, a "tendency towards mutual suspicion between lesbians and gay men."

In 1983, the relatively young network of LGBTQ choral societies took a big leap forward into visibility. The first National Gay Choral Festival was scheduled for September, to be held in Manhattan at Lincoln Center's Alice Tully Hall, as prestigious a cultural venue as existed in the United States. Almost seven hundred singers from eleven choruses performed at the festival. Artemis was the only group of women among them. "Come Out and Sing Together," as the festival was titled, stretched over three days. At a time when AIDS was beginning to ravage the world of gay and bisexual men in large American cities, and when media coverage strengthened the most negative stereotypes of homosexuality, the choral festival provided a much-needed counterpoint. By 1986, when a second national choral festival was held, "women's participation had increased five-fold," according to a report in the Artemis Papers.

The work of Artemis, as well as that of other lesbian choruses that sprang up in these years, did have an impact on the gender dynamics of these musical networks. Testimonials from a national conference of the Gay and Lesbian Association of Choruses (GALA Choruses) held in Minneapolis in 1986 document the progress. "I went to Minneapolis with more than a slight case of negativity," one lesbian wrote after the event. "I had prepared myself to grin and bear it . . . Never did I dream that I would come to feel such a close and compassionate bond with 1200 other singers, most of them men." Another woman wrote, "while the membership and leadership are overwhelmingly male, most seem supportive or even enthusiastic about recruiting women's choruses . . . Anything is possible." At the GALA Choruses conference in Vancouver the following year, panels titled "Women and Men Together in GALA" and "A Dialogue on Women's Issues in GALA" brought matters of sexism and gender parity into the open.

Besides challenging the gender dynamics of this larger queer musical world that was growing in the 1980s, a group like Artemis also helped build a stronger sense of community and shared identity among lesbians. Artemis Singers performed several times a year in Chicago. Sometimes the events were consciously political, as when they did a benefit concert to raise money for *Gay Community News*, a Boston-based LGBTQ weekly with very progressive politics, and one for the National Organization for Women and its campaign for the Equal Rights Amendment. Sometimes the events were benefits to support Artemis, none of whose members were paid, but for whom the expense of traveling to festivals and purchasing music could be costly. In 1986, Artemis had $4,600 in its bank account, not an insignificant sum for those times and a sign of the popularity of its public events.

I am not sure how one measures the impact of a group like Artemis. But coming across comments like the concert was "a smashing success" or an event was filled with "magical moments" certainly suggests a collective power to the experience. It was not uncommon for two hundred to three hundred people to attend these musical events in various community venues. Artemis sang music ranging from sixteenth-century madrigals by an Italian woman composer to the contemporary music of figures like Holly Near and Dolly Parton. Within the larger group, its six-women "Barbershop Queertet" was especially popular. One measure of the appeal of Artemis, perhaps, is the fact that in 2019, almost four decades after it was founded, the Artemis Singers were still performing. They still had the power to bring people together and spread joy among their audiences. Many—indeed, most—LGBTQ organizations cannot claim such a long and productive life.

22

Printing Our Way to Freedom: The Metis Press

Sometime in 1973, in the months when I was first making my way into the world of LGBTQ activism and sharing my excitement about it with almost everyone, a friend gave me a copy of a novel she had just read. *Rubyfruit Jungle* was written by Rita Mae Brown, who had been deeply involved in New York City in the first wave of militant lesbian feminism that exploded at the end of the 1960s. My friend Mimi assured me that I would like the book, but "like" proved to be quite the understatement. I was completely captivated by it and raced through the whole novel in two sittings. The very little bit of gay literature that I had read up to that point was mired in a world of suicides and other forms of tragedy. Not this one. The heroine, Molly Bolt, was a take-no-prisoners fighter who was not, under any circumstances, going to let society constrain her from reaching her dreams and living a life of her own design. I alternated between gasping at her audacity and cheering her on as she made her way through a New York in the 1960s that was not exactly welcoming to an out-front lesbian. Reading it, I found myself thinking that the revolution was on its way and might arrive as early as next week.

Rita Mae Brown went on to write a stream of books, published by mainstream presses, and *Rubyfruit Jungle* went through many print-ings, perhaps becoming the best-selling lesbian novel of the 1970s

The research for this essay is based on the records of the Metis Press Collective, Gerber/Hart Library and Archives.

and 1980s. But the version that Mimi gave me was produced by a small publisher based in Vermont, by the name of Daughters Press. I did not realize it at the time, but Daughters was just one of many feminist presses coming into existence in the 1970s with the purpose of making sure that the voices of a new generation of women writers would be heard. By 1976, three years after Daughters published *Rubyfruit*, feminist publishing had become enough of a movement that a "Women in Print" conference convened at a campsite outside Omaha, Nebraska. One hundred and thirty women attended from across the United States; eighty groups were represented. According to an account that appeared in *Big Mama Rag*, a feminist periodical from that era, "a feeling of sisterhood and admiration prevailed."

Two of the women who attended were Christine Johnson and Amy Christine Straayer, a couple who, along with another friend, Barbara Emrys, had just begun a publishing venture of their own in Chicago. As Straayer described the beginnings of Metis Press, "None of us knew how to print. None of us had any time, any money. At the end of nine months, none of us had any energy left. But we'd printed our first big job." Throughout its years, Metis was kept alive by "lesbian womyn who donate their labor and time . . . We each work outside jobs." Even after a decade of operation, during which Metis published a number of books and journals, a press release celebrating its tenth anniversary described the situation like this: "We still ain't got no money, but we sure have printed a whole lot of everything *but* money."

As with so many other lesbian-feminist projects of the 1970s, a sense of almost missionary zeal brought Metis into existence and kept it alive for many years. The women involved wanted to create "an alternative women's literary network" to compensate for the neglect of women writers generally, and lesbian writers in particular, by the mainstream publishing industry. "We believe in publishing that tells our stories, that helps to end the censorship of our experience. Our goal is to build a feminist publishing house that is a community."

Fiction and poetry were the primary works that Metis published.

Though none of their books had anything like the success of *Ruby-fruit Jungle*, some did arouse enthusiasm in readers and went through multiple printings. Perhaps the most successful was *Wild Women Don't Get the Blues*, a collection of short stories by Barbara Emrys, one of the founders of the press. Metis also took on the task of printing *Black Maria*, a feminist literary journal put together in Chicago that began in the early 1970s and lasted well into the 1980s. *Black Maria* published everything from poetry, memoir, and short stories to historical episodes of women's resistance to oppression and contemporary accounts of feminist activism. Like Metis, the journal operated on a shoestring budget. Its income in 1981 was less than $1,500. But it had the support of high-profile writers like Ntozake Shange, who submitted poems to it.

What most impressed me about the work of Metis was the evidence attesting to the wide reach of this feminist publishing network in the 1970s and early 1980s. Letters arrived from across the United States from women writers who had heard about Metis and were inquiring as to whether it might publish their novel or short stories. Especially after Metis released in 1979 *A Book of One's Own: A Guide to Self-Publishing*, correspondence flowed in from feminist bookstore owners and other small presses. From Arizona to Oregon to Connecticut came requests to carry the books that Metis was publishing. And, significantly, knowledge of Metis had a global reach. The press received inquiries from Britain, South Africa, India, and Australia. An offer came from Montreal to translate some of its work into French.

Members of this world of feminist publishing made a conscious effort to build and keep strong the networks that would sustain them. There was a gathering of women in alternative publishing at the National Women's Studies Association Conference in 1979. Two years later, a second nationwide "Women in Print" conference convened in Washington, DC. The following year, midwesterners involved in such publishing ventures gathered for several days to share experiences.

Significantly, by the early 1980s, a different tone seemed to prevail. Reagan was president. A religious right was visibly organizing against key feminist issues, like reproductive rights, and against the LGBTQ community generally. A July 1981 mailing announcing the second "Women in Print" conference forthrightly declared: "The rationale for the conference is survival. The survival of the women's movement, as of any revolutionary movement, depends directly on that of our communications network. In threatening times we must strengthen ourselves and one another." The following year, after the Midwest regional "Women in Print" gathering, the Metis collective wrote and circulated an account with a similar theme. While the gathering was "very stimulating and quite successful in many ways," it reported, the overarching theme was "survival." It went on to elaborate: "Survival in the financial and political climate of today, yes, but more importantly (and even alarmingly) our survival from within the lesbian/feminist and feminist literary network. In short, how to help womyn see and feel the extreme importance of supporting womyn-produced work by consciously seeking out womyn's print shops, publishers, and bookstores." Ironically, to the degree that feminist presses were successful in publishing and promoting work by women, they were opening the doors of mainstream trade publishers to women writers. These publishing houses had far more resources to promote and distribute books. They could sell books at lower prices than the small feminist endeavors.

The Metis papers at Gerber/Hart do not provide definitive information on the precise circumstances that led it, and *Black Maria*, finally to cease operating. The *Black Maria* collective, which never included more than a handful of women, managed to put together sixteen issues of the journal between 1971 and 1985. It disbanded the following year but reconstituted itself in 1987 as "a very organized and motivated group," according to one of its grant applications. But no evidence exists of the collective succeeding in producing another issue. And materials in the Metis papers end in 1987. One senses that, by the second half of the 1980s, the intense energy that had propelled a variety of lesbian-feminist ventures into existence in the early 1970s was dissipating. The always scarce financial resources, the double load of work that members of these collectives faced, and the fact that, for some lesbians at least, mainstream opportunities were opening together took their toll on these movement-oriented impulses.

As is true of so many archival collections at Gerber/Hart, the Metis Press papers are a treasure trove of materials that go beyond the specific work of Metis and *Black Maria*. Immersed as these women were in the world of feminist publishing, they naturally came into possession of a host of feminist publications—especially newsletters, magazines, and newspapers—that were being produced by community activists around the country. Some of the titles capture the rebellious spirit of 1970s feminism: *Lesbian Contradiction: A Journal of Irreverent Feminism*, published in Seattle; *Lunatic Fringe: A Newsletter for Separatist, Anarchist, and Radical Feminist Lesbians of Chicago*; and *Hag Rag*, produced in Wisconsin and specializing in "New Rage Thinking." Reading these publications today, more than a generation later, offers sharp insights into the lesbian-feminist movement of the 1970s and early 1980s.

23
Picturing Lesbian History: The Passion of Janet Soule

As the stories of the Lesbian Community Center, the Artemis Singers, and Metis Press in the previous essays suggest, the 1970s and 1980s were decades in which the push to establish lesbian and woman-centered spaces was strong. The sexist gendering of the economy and of public life, not only in heterosexual America but in the gay world as well, meant that in this new era of lesbian-feminist resistance, creating and supporting a wide range of places that were woman-centered was a major priority for many lesbians.

The work of Janet Soule provides additional insight into this impulse. In the late 1970s and 1980s, Soule earned her living primarily by working as a cataloger at Northwestern University Library. But her deep familiarity with the world of books and publishing also led Soule to use her spare time to advance lesbian and feminist projects. In the 1970s, she was part of the small collective of lesbians that ran Metis Press. She was also variously the proprietor of Sandpiper Books, a woman-focused mail-order book service, and of Woman Wild: Treasures by Women, a gallery and gift shop. Located on Clark Street in Andersonville, a neighborhood that was beginning to gather a concentration of lesbians, Woman Wild sold arts and crafts made by women from around the country.

These businesses were themselves vehicles that advanced what

The research for this essay is based on the Janet Soule Papers, Gerber/Hart Library and Archives.

seemed to be her greatest passion: producing an illustrated calendar on lesbian history. In 1984, she completed the first of these. *Tracking Our Way through Time: A Lesbian Herstory Calendar/Journal* was printed by Metis Press. In 1990, when the documentation in her papers ends, she was in the midst of gathering materials to produce a second volume. Whether the second was ever completed remains unclear.

Soule's own words give some sense of the power that history had for many feminist lesbians of this era. She described the first calendar as "260 spiral-bound pages of facts/photos/quotes/graphics documenting Lesbian herstory. Designed as a journal and engagement calendar, this treasure will create daily lesbian energy." The idea for the project came when, looking through the December 1979 issue of *Ms.* magazine in Northwestern's library, she saw that none of the women's calendars for 1980 that *Ms.* reviewed were lesbian-focused. Writing personally in the preface, Soule explained that "the vision that has literally propelled me through the waves of work is the knowledge that the visibility that this work could bring us is the kind of visibility that will keep us alive."

Soule's papers provide a vivid sense of the effort to find, claim, and circulate a lesbian herstory during decades—the 1970s and 1980s—when lesbians were almost completely invisible in mainstream popular culture and media. In her determination to gather sufficient material to transform her dream of a calendar-journal into a reality, Soule searched for information relentlessly. Besides the research she did in the Northwestern library, she sent out a large number of "Sharing Womyn" letters to activists, to lesbian publications, and to the few individuals who were known at the time to be engaged in the recovery of lesbian history. What she collected offers insight into the work of lesbians and other feminists to make herstory and woman-centered cultural expression more accessible. Though put together and published by Soule, *Tracking Our Way through Time* was very much a collective effort.

As a resource for herself and others, Soule both collected and compiled a set of bibliographies on a range of topics. She had bibliographies on history, mythology, theology, and Jewish women. There is a twenty-two-page bibliography of literature by black women. Soule seemed particularly interested in the subject of religion, perhaps hoping to challenge conventional assumptions about Christianity's condemnation of homosexuality. She gathered pamphlets and clipped and saved many articles from the Christian press during these years. One of the most substantial items was *Homosexuality: A Selected Bibliography for Christian Counselors*. Duane Harbin, who compiled it, also provided annotations for the entries. It is an invaluable resource for assessing the state of religious thinking in these years.

Soule made use of other resources as well. Marie Kuda was a community-based historian in Chicago. She put together a slide lecture on lesbian herstory, "From Boston Marriages to the Tell-All 1970s," that she presented many times across the Midwest and elsewhere. Kuda made her materials available to Soule. Judith Schwarz was an East Coast independent historian who worked closely with the Lesbian Herstory Archives in New York. She was publishing historical essays in lesbian and feminist publications as early as the 1970s. Soule was in contact with her as well and used her research as a source. Soule sought from community-based researchers their work in progress on lesbian history, and she amassed a set of unpublished papers. She also compulsively clipped and saved articles from the gay and lesbian press of these years, which occasionally published explorations of lesbian history.

Tracking Our Way through Time is rich with inspiring pictures of lesbian heroes and of activism at work. It provides bits and pieces of the past as one moves through the months of the year. Soule includes examples of Native American life from the nineteenth century. African American lesbians and Third World women's activism are well represented. But the calendar also inadvertently reveals how little lesbian history was accessible in the early 1980s, even with Soule's wide-ranging effort to collect it. The vast majority of entries are from the 1970s. Soule documents events of broad consequence, such as the first national conference of lesbians, held at

UCLA in April of 1973, that brought together 1,700 lesbians from forty-one states—without question the largest event of its kind ever convened up to that point. And she also documents the local, such as the testimony of E. Kitch Childs, an African American lesbian psychologist who, in October 1973, testified before the Judiciary Committee of the Chicago City Council in favor of bills that would have prohibited discrimination based on sexual orientation and would have repealed a city law that banned "cross-dressing." In that sense, the calendar functions today as a piece of history itself. It can serve as a source and a guide for some of the key events and individuals in lesbian history from that decade.

But it is not only the content of the calendar that makes Soule's work a resource for learning about the 1970s. She also gathered material about women-owned enterprises. For instance, in 1982, Women's Bookstore of Worchester, Massachusetts, conducted a survey of women's bookstores in the United States and Canada. It found that lesbian literature was among the strongest sales areas in these businesses, that the primary motive behind these enterprises was "political," that almost all were near a college or university, and that sole ownership businesses were more likely to succeed than collectives. On a more sobering note, store owners reported that the larger the lesbian percentage of customers, the less likely a business was to remain viable. Soule also gathered evidence about the efforts among lesbians to form rural land collectives. A first attempt to identify such groups located ten of them in 1976. By the time of a follow-up search in 1983, almost fifty were identified in twenty-four states, with land ownership exceeding three thousand acres. One near the Illinois River promised visitors a secluded, scenic retreat. Taken together, the materials Soule collected as she sought to put together her calendar provide valuable evidence of the widespread efforts to create and sustain lesbian-identified and woman-centered spaces in the 1970s and 1980s.

As happens so often in archival research, I came upon one document in particular that called into question certain assumptions I held. One of the bibliographies that Soule received was simply titled

"Women." It was an especially thick compilation of work by and about women that was produced by the Alabama Public Library Service in conjunction with the celebration of International Women's Year in Alabama in 1977. Its existence challenged my sense of a geographic divide between areas that were receptive to feminism and areas opposed to it. Here was a resource produced by a state agency in the "Deep South" that was designed to highlight women's accomplishments and raise public consciousness. History can be more complex than some of us, including me, assume it to be.

24

Lesbian Chicago: Striving for Visibility

One of the more exciting outcomes of researching history is the way patterns can emerge. At some point, a common theme surfaces, and it leads to a deeper understanding of the period. Suddenly, instead of simply adding to my factual knowledge, a "truth" about the historical era that I am researching asserts itself.

Looked at together, the research into Janet Soule, the Lesbian Community Center, and the Artemis Singers produced such a recognition. In each case, the theme of invisibility surfaced. In the 1970s and early 1980s, lesbian activists with very different goals—researching history, establishing a community center, making music—were nonetheless echoing a similar concern. In Chicago, many lesbians felt that, as a group, they were largely invisible, and the quest for visibility pushed them to take action.

Unfortunately, that nagging sense of being invisible and marginalized still had not vanished as the 1980s came to an end. Between 1990 and 1993, a group of lesbians in Chicago worked very hard to try, once again, to establish a lesbian community center. The "Lesbian Chicago" collection at Gerber/Hart, which was donated by Veronica Drake, offers a view into those efforts. Drake had been a member of ACT UP (AIDS Coalition to Unleash Power) in the late 1980s; she was involved for several years with Horizons

The research for this essay is based on the Veronica Drake Papers, Gerber/Hart Library and Archives.

Community Services, which aimed to be responsive to the whole LGBTQ community; and she served as a Midwest delegate on the 1993 March on Washington Steering Committee. Her papers place front and center the theme of invisibility and the felt need to challenge it. Its prominence is sobering when one considers the vital role that lesbians played in the activism around AIDS in the 1980s and early 1990s. But in the public eye, the AIDS epidemic was so male identified that it may ironically have reinforced lesbian invisibility despite their heavy involvement in the community response to this tragic health crisis.

The story begins in January 1990. Seventy-five women attended an open meeting to discuss what the organizers of the meeting described as "refining the lesbian agenda." Among the key themes articulated at the meeting was a strongly felt need for "women-only space" and the simultaneously harsh reality of "money and women's general lack thereof." By evening's end, there was "virtually unanimous agreement that a major concern of the women's community is lesbian invisibility." A decision was made to meet again in February. But the collection is then largely silent about the activities that occur for the remainder of the year and into the first part of 1991. A loose-knit group of lesbian activists did coalesce and continue to meet. A *Lesbian Chicago Newsletter* from September 1990 announced that the group would formalize its structure at a meeting later that month. An undefined fund-raiser at the beginning of September raised $833, and another fund-raiser—a fall dance— was coming up in October.

The harsh reality of limited resources was making it hard to function completely independently, and so, in September 1991, the group signed a letter of agreement with the Rodde Center and its director, Al Wardell. The Rodde Center, named after a popular gay bartender who was murdered in 1977, had existed as a community space in different locations for almost a dozen years. In 1990, it had moved to a large five-thousand-square-foot rented space at 4753 Broadway, in the Uptown neighborhood, a low-rent district on Chicago's North Side. The agreement with Rodde allowed Lesbian Chicago to use three rooms rent free on Monday evenings from five to eleven, until the end of June 1992. At that point, both groups would take stock of how the relationship was going. Lesbian Chicago was seeing this as a temporary way station, one that would provide a modicum of stability, give them visibility, and allow them to begin shaping a role in the community and creating a set of programs to serve that community of women-loving women. A meeting that key members held in early December 1991 recommended forming a board of directors whose sole purpose would be fund-raising so that, in time, Lesbian Chicago would be able to purchase a building and become a stable presence in Chicago.

The women involved in the project proved very capable of keeping their rooms filled with activities for the evening that was allotted to them. The Artemis Singers gave a performance to celebrate the opening. Marie Kuda, a community-based historian, presented illustrated lectures of lesbian herstory. Lesbian Chicago hosted several organizations and support groups, among them BLABS, Black Lesbians about Bonding in Sisterhood; Lesbians over 40; Lesbians with Disabilities and Chronic Illnesses; and the Lesbian Community Cancer Project. It also offered the community a range of social and educational activities, including game nights, movies, craft work, health programming, and a "Let's Talk about Sex" discussion group. "Open Mike" nights and dances were held periodically to bring together large numbers of women and to raise money for a hoped-for independent lesbian community center.

By spring 1992, when it was time to renegotiate the agreement with the Rodde Center, the women of Lesbian Chicago had decided that they were still committed to the goal of a lesbian-identified space. Rather than paying rent to the Rodde Center, even if it would bring greater access to its space, Lesbian Chicago made the decision to work with the Lesbian Community Cancer Project in order to have a woman-centered location. Together they rented a building at 1902 West Montrose, a mile and a half from the Rodde Center. They named it "Pat Parker Place," in honor of the African American poet who had recently died of cancer. By day it would serve the clients of LCCP. In the evenings it would support a broad range of lesbian-oriented groups and activities sponsored by Lesbian Chicago. Its opening event on September 20, 1992, featured an art exhibit by lesbians of color.

Exciting as the move to a space of their own was, the Lesbian Chicago initiative continued to face serious challenges. In the months before moving out of the Rodde Center, Lesbian Chicago had less than $500 in its bank account. A board meeting held soon after the move emphasized the need for "new bodies so our old ones don't burn out." Participants also acknowledged that "our lack of cash is a serious problem" and that, despite all the work participants were doing, Lesbian Chicago still needed "better name recognition." The mission statement it issued in October 1992 projected a tone of confidence. It declared that "Lesbian Chicago is the Chicago area's *only* lesbian community center. Its mission is to build a culturally diverse, disability-sensitive, women-only safe-space to develop organizations, share information, develop networks, socialize, and increase the visibility of lesbians in the community-at-large." But, just a few months later, in a tone now bordering on desperation, Lesbian Chicago's Executive Committee laid out a series of compelling questions for which it did not yet have answers: "What *are* we doing at this stage in our growth? Are we being effective? Are we addressing the needs of the community? . . . What *should* we be doing at this stage in our growth? . . . How do we become a moving force, a centerpiece in the community? What kinds of things should we be doing to get name recognition?"

Veronica Drake's papers continue to provide information about the work of Lesbian Chicago through the spring of 1993. But then they go silent. There are no more newsletters, no more minutes of board meetings, no more coverage in the local press. Did Veronica Drake, who donated the papers, move on to other activities? How much longer was Lesbian Chicago able to continue? The project of building and sustaining centers was not easy even for the broader LGBTQ community. The Rodde Center, which initially housed Lesbian Chicago, only lasted for another two or three years.

Whatever the particular fate of the Lesbian Chicago project, it remained true that, into the 1990s, lesbians in Chicago continued to come together in various groupings to provide support and community for one another in women-loving-women spaces. And, as the case of Amigas Latinas will reveal, that impulse continued into the new century.

25

We Are Family: The Birth of Amigas Latinas

It started as a simple Sunday brunch. A group of friends—Evette Cardona, Mona Noriega, Aurora Pineda, Lydia Vega, and a few others—got together at one of their homes to talk and share personal stories. Without quite planning it, one brunch led to another. Each gathering was followed by a next one at which new faces appeared. Soon, the women began showing up at community events together and organizing activities of their own. Twenty years later, what had started as a small informal social group had changed forever the public face of the LGBTQ community in Chicago.

That first Sunday brunch evolved over time into Amigas Latinas, an organization of women-loving women of Latinx heritage. It began in 1995, not long after the militant direct-action tactics of ACT UP and Queer Nation had brought unprecedented attention to the LGBTQ community and its issues. At the time of that first brunch, AIDS was still proving devastatingly destructive, as the caseload and number of deaths continued to increase, and the epidemic was disproportionately affecting Latino men. Except for a small number of individuals, Latina lesbians as a group were not a noticeably visible presence either in the LGBTQ community or in the larger Latinx community in Chicago.

Twenty years later, in 2015, much had changed. Illinois had

Research for this essay is based on the papers of Amigas Latinas, Gerber/Hart Library and Archives.

amended its civil rights statutes to prohibit discrimination based on sexual orientation. Marriage equality had been achieved in Illinois. Out-of-the-closet Latina lesbians filled several significant leadership roles and worked with a large number of community-based organizations on a broad range of issues. The twelve boxes of Amigas Latinas Papers detail the story of how this Sunday brunch coalesced into something much larger and how this pioneering organization made its influence widely felt.

A key document brings to life the group's earliest years and how it evolved. In 2002, Sylvia Puente organized focus groups of Amigas Latinas members and conducted a series of interviews with them. Some had heard about the group through a friend or acquaintance and had their first connection to it by attending a Sunday brunch and then returning again and again. A few remarked that "they did not know anyone when they pursued their involvement with Amigas Latinas." Many had maintained discretion about their sexual identity and had never told another soul. The group was "the first place where they felt they could be both"—Latina and lesbian. "I had to be true to myself, my life had been a lie," one woman declared. Repeatedly, interviewees told Puente that "Amigas Latinas means 'family' . . . Amigas is like an extended family." The comparison with family emerges as especially significant because many did not yet feel able to come out to their families of birth, while others had experienced rejection by family when they did come out. Amigas "remedied this isolation." It became "a place of 'chosen family'" where every gathering served to affirm that "it is 'ok' to be a Latina lesbian."

For the first two years or so, the monthly Sunday brunch was the core activity of the group. But an important turning point came in 1998. The National Latino/a Lesbian and Gay Organization (LLEGÓ) decided to hold its national conference in Chicago for the first time. With another Chicago-based organization, the Association of Latino Men in Action (ALMA), the women of Amigas Latinas worked on the local organizing committee to help make the event a success. It led Amigas to form for the first time a steering committee that held meetings independently of the Sunday brunches. The deep involvement in LLEGÓ's national conference, which focused on political and social change and on movement building, pushed some of the women in Amigas toward a more collective activist vision.

By the time Puente conducted her interviews in 2002, Amigas had become more visible. It marched as a group in the annual Puerto Rican Parade and in the Mexican Independence Day Parade. It participated in the Dyke March that occurred each June. It had a float in Chicago's yearly Pride Parade. It launched a scholarship fund for young queer Latinas and held a public dinner and award ceremony. It organized a family picnic so that mothers and their children would have a safe space to socialize and an opportunity to meet other queer Latina families. It began doing trainings on lesbian issues for other community organizations, like Mujeres Latinas en Accion. Amigas began applying for, and receiving, small foundation grants to help finance its work. Through all this, the monthly Sunday brunch remained a constant, the place where new women could connect with others and become part of a social circle that reflected back to them their multiple identities. Taken together, these activities and others led many of Puente's interviewees to insist that "there is a growing need for Amigas Latinas . . . there is no other organization that serves the community the way that Amigas does." They wanted Amigas "to be more visible . . . there is a need to provide more services and support groups," particularly in Spanish. Overall, there was an expectation that Amigas should be "moving to become a more formal organization."

Over the next couple of years that expectation was fulfilled. Amigas launched its own webpage. It received 501(c)(3) status as a not-for-profit organization. It expanded enormously the kind of social gatherings it sponsored in the course of a month. Besides the brunches, there were family movie nights and bowling nights, holiday parties for children, family picnics in warmer weather, culture nights, game nights, and discussion groups on a broad range of topics. These expanded social activities were consistent with the way Amigas came into being. But the survey that Puente conducted also suggested a desire among many for the group to have an impact in the world of political action and community organizing. That kind of growth seemed "inevitable and necessary." Yet if Amigas moved in that direction, some wondered if it would "lose its family atmosphere." It was a concern that many expressed. Would the safety and the relaxed informality of most of its gatherings be sacrificed to the cause of movement activism? Would there still be a place for those who simply needed to know that there were others like themselves, whose lives could be changed through the chance interactions that occurred over a meal eaten while sitting on a living room couch?

26

Our Legacy Lives On: Amigas Latinas as an Activist Force

Historical research has a cumulative effect. Each box of documents will add something to the sum of one's knowledge—another event, another actor, a new point of view. But occasionally researching history offers much more. It allows one to pull together a set of themes and patterns that characterize the broader panorama. Suddenly, one sees with clarity several key elements that distinguish a period of history, elements that have surfaced again and again as one explores the past.

The history of Amigas Latinas took on that quality for me. Its evolution seemed to confirm a series of conclusions that had been dangling in front of me: that the boundary between what we think of as "social" and "political," between socializing and working to make change, is actually quite porous, and the former can often lead organically to the latter; that the need for women-only space remained powerful across several decades; and that the AIDS epidemic that arose in the 1980s had the power to provoke change of all sorts, in unexpected ways, well beyond that decade.

In the undergraduate course that I taught for many years in LGBTQ studies, I repeatedly used the phrase "AIDS changes everything" when we came to the 1980s and discussed the onset of the epidemic. AIDS dramatically escalated the urgency of political orga-

Research for this essay is based on the Amigas Latinas Records, Gerber/Hart Library and Archives.

nizing within the LGBTQ community. Suddenly, activism became a matter not simply of sexual and personal freedom, but of life and death. AIDS led to many more individuals coming out. It brought into existence a wide range of service organizations to fill the gap created by the mainstream health care industry's early neglect of people with AIDS. This in turn strengthened the community bonds among individuals. And, as the epidemic continued and as government finally began providing funds to fight its spread and care for those who were sick, many LGBTQ organizations suddenly found themselves with the financial resources to hire staff and more effectively pursue their mission.

How does the story of Amigas Latinas confirm this interpretive lens? The first important step of Amigas toward activism came in 1998, when it helped organize the national conference in Chicago of LLEGÓ, the National Latino/a Lesbian and Gay Organization. Founded as part of the activism generated by the 1987 National March on Washington for Lesbian and Gay Rights, LLEGÓ by the early 1990s found itself able to qualify for federal funds directed toward organizations that worked on AIDS prevention in racial and ethnic minority communities. AIDS education efforts within Latinx communities provided the resources that allowed LLEGÓ to do LGBTQ organizing more generally. By the mid-1990s, LLEGÓ had ties with perhaps as many as two hundred queer Latinx organizations across the United States. By volunteering to be part of the Chicago-based local organizing committee for the 1998 national gathering of LLEGÓ and affiliated organizations, members of Amigas Latinas found themselves deep inside a large network of activists. To be surrounded for the first time by hundreds of other community organizers who were both Latinx and LGBTQ had the power to be a life-changing experience.

The connection that Amigas established with LLEGÓ continued to have a ripple effect on the women in Chicago. In 2002, the same year that Amigas convened focus groups that highlighted a desire to make a bigger impact on society, it was one of only three local groups invited by LLEGÓ to participate in "Proyecto BASTA!," the first national effort to address the issue of domestic violence within the "women-loving-women" Latina population. The topic had been surfacing in the support groups and informal discussions that Amigas sponsored, and it eagerly took advantage of the opportunity to engage in this effort. Establishing a close working relationship with Mujeres Latinas en Accion, perhaps the largest organization in the Midwest that worked on the issue within the Latinx community, members of Amigas began offering trainings and information on the experience of domestic violence among Latina lesbians. It also began providing referrals within its network of lesbians to those women who needed counseling and support. The project led to the publication of "BASTA! 2004: Committed to Ending Violence against Women," which offered information about the factors leading to domestic violence, the kind of help that was available to women targeted by abuse, and how individuals and organizations might provide these women with assistance. The work on domestic violence brought into bold relief that the "social" and the "political" were not disconnected.

As Amigas took on this issue, it began to address as well other pressing issues that were surfacing. For instance, many of the women who came to the brunches were mothers. They had stories to share of the challenges that being both a mother and a lesbian posed for themselves and their children. In 2004, Amigas moved beyond simply having picnics for mothers and their children and formed the first Spanish-language PFLAG (Parents and Friends of Lesbians and Gays) group in greater Chicago. PFLAG, a national organization, was well-established in the Chicago metropolitan area, with a number of chapters. It was deeply engaged with a range of issues affecting the LGBTQ community, especially involving schools and how LGBTQ youth were treated. Not surprisingly, a couple of years after Amigas formed the PFLAG chapter, it also established Amiguitas, the first group for young queer Latinas. Amiguitas provided a space for youth to explore their identities, meet other girls and young women, and have a support network.

Motivated by this plunge into more activist endeavors, at the end of 2006 Amigas launched Proyecto Latina, the first broad-based survey of the Latina lesbian, bisexual, transgender, queer, and questioning population in the greater Chicago area. The survey highlighted several issues, but one that stood out dramatically was immigration. A number of the women in Amigas and among the survey participants were immigrants; many others were the children of immigrants. US immigration law had a long history of being anti-LGBTQ. Even as the formal legal structure of federal policy changed, those who fell within the spectrum of nonheterosexual and non-gender-binary identities felt themselves vulnerable. As right-wing organizations fanned the flames of hatred in the twenty-first century toward what conservatives described as "illegal immigrants," the defense of immigrants grew more and more urgent. Members of Amigas helped form the Chicago LGBTQ Immigrant Alliance (CLIA). It was designed to address "the disproportionate impact of harmful immigration policy upon the LGBTQ communities." In taking on this issue directly, Amigas sought "to integrate LGBT concerns into the mainstream immigration reform community and immigration concerns into the LGBT community."

With community services, education, and political activism moving to center stage, Amigas expanded in size. Its financial records show that in its 2004–5 fiscal year, it raised a bit more than $14,000. Just two years later, its revenues had risen to over $54,000. The growth came both from its ability to receive foundation grants, now that it was more than simply a social group, and from the expansion of a pool of individual donors that its growing visibility enabled. In 2006, Amigas hired its first paid staffer. It began partnering with the Center on Halsted, Chicago's LGBTQ community center, on youth services and other issues. And the center delegated space to it.

As issues like immigration and the needs of queer youth became core parts of its mission, it might seem that the need for Amigas to remain a separate and distinct organization might have faded. Why not merge with other organizations that were addressing these concerns? But, as other stories in this collection suggest, throughout the 1970s and 1980s, the impulse for lesbians to create and maintain women-only spaces had been strong. Even as community centers, health care initiatives, and history projects were established in the LGBTQ community, groups of lesbians continued to support autonomous organizing efforts. The founding of Amigas Latinas in 1995 and its growth in the early years of this century suggest that the need for that kind of safe space was still compelling.

Across the many movements for social change and social justice, very few organizations last for more than a generation. In 2015, twenty years after the first Sunday brunch, Amigas Latinas announced that it was folding. The announcement elicited both declarations of sadness that the organization was closing down and words of praise about its powerful impact over the years. In an interview about the closing, Evette Cardona, one of the founders of Amigas Latinas, put its history in perspective. "So many things were different 20 years ago," she said. "When we first started Amigas we could have never envisioned marriage or two women choosing to have children together and being out as a family. We couldn't have envisioned all the Latina queer women who are in positions of power and influence as they are now, whether it's Mona [Noriega] working for the City of Chicago [as chair of the Commission on Human Relations], me in my job [at the Polk Brothers Foundation] or Alicia [Vega] being the vice-president of youth development at the Boys and Girls Club of Chicago." Summarizing what had changed in the course of two decades, Cardona concluded: "That single need for one space where all Latina lesbians could gather isn't true anymore because we are everywhere." Alicia Vega, another core member of Amigas, described the closing this way: "Amigas has made an impact on so many lives and its impact will live on in the lives of those it touched. The official closing of the organization is administrative; the legacy of Amigas Latinas lives on."

27

Challenging a Color Line: Black and White Men Together

As historians research the past, many of us often operate with a set of categories that help to sort and divide the past into neatly organized separate boxes. There are histories of politics and movement activism; of social life and community; of culture and artistic production. But life is not always so neatly segmented. Political activism can be a force for building community. Socializing in bars sometimes became the setting for mobilizing people, most famously at the Stonewall Inn in 1969. And cultural creativity can help articulate political grievances and rouse people to action.

The haziness of history's boundaries came home to me as I explored the history of Black and White Men Together. Two Chicagoans, Ken Allen and Wendell Reid, were especially active in the organization. Their papers at Gerber/Hart cover the decades of the 1980s and 1990s, when the organization was growing and in its most dynamic phase.

Black and White Men Together formed in San Francisco in the spring of 1980. By the time it held its first conference in San Francisco during Pride Month in 1981, there already were ten chapters, stretching from cities in California and Arizona to Missouri, Florida, North Carolina, Pennsylvania, and Michigan. Three hundred men attended that first national convention. By 1987, at least sev-

The research for this essay is based on the Ken Allen Papers and Wendell Reid Papers, Gerber/Hart Library and Archives.

enteen chapters were regularly producing newsletters, some of which were quite substantial. By the early 1990s, when BWMT had passed the ten-year mark in its history, it claimed over one thousand members. There were chapters in nineteen states, and many of them were located in cities not generally thought of as hubs of gay male life—among them, Hartford, Connecticut; Youngstown, Ohio; and Louisville, Kentucky. By 1995, when it held its fifteenth national convention, it proudly announced that BWMT had "multiplied into a national web of dozens of chapters."

From the outside, BWMT was often perceived as what today one might describe as a "meet-up" group for gay men whose sexual attractions crossed a color line. And, undoubtedly, it did serve that purpose, filling a need that was all the more pressing because evidence abounds that, in the 1970s, many gay bars implemented policies of excluding African American men by demanding extra forms of identification. BWMT provided safe spaces for interracial socializing. Chapters often met in larger regional gatherings as well, which helped break through the isolation that interracial couples in smaller communities were likely to experience. But social ties and sexual connections were by no means the whole story. The socializing in turn helped build broad networks that facilitated organization building as well as campaigns for institutional change and community education.

Evidence abounds that activist motivations were strong in BWMT. At its tenth anniversary convention, held in San Francisco in June 1990, keynote speakers included Urvashi Vaid, executive director of the National Gay and Lesbian Task Force and a highly visible advocate for multi-issue, multiracial LGBTQ organizing; Paulette Goodman, the national president of Parents and Friends of Lesbians and Gays; and Renee McCoy, the founding pastor of a Metropolitan Community Church congregation in Harlem and an executive director of the National Coalition of Black Lesbians and Gays. Workshops included "How Does the Media Cover Our Issues," "Empowering Our Lesbian/Gay Youth," and "Beyond the Bar: Political Activism in the '90s." The programs of the 1991 and

1992 national conventions, held in Detroit and Dallas, respectively, provide even more evidence of political consciousness and intentions. The choice of keynote speakers helped raise the profile of black LGBTQ activists. They included Perry Watkins, an African American soldier who was one of the main individuals challenging the military's exclusion policy; Keith St. John, a member of the City Council of Albany, New York, and the first openly gay black man elected to public office; Mandy Carter, one of the most politically progressive grassroots community organizers in the US and whose activist roots were in the peace movement; and Marjorie Hill, the director of New York City's Office for Lesbian and Gay Community Concerns. Many of the workshops at these conferences were unmistakably activist in their focus: "You Can't Fight AIDS from the Closet," "Lesbians and Gays of Color as a Political Force in the '92 Elections," "A History of Gay Rights," "Anti-Gay Violence," and "Establishing Your Own HIV/AIDS Agency." The political orientation of these national convocations comes through clearly in the messages that keynote speakers delivered. For instance, Keith Boykin, who was a media advisor in the Clinton administration, gave a speech described as "very much a wake-up call" about the threat posed by anti-LGBTQ forces. Echoing a poem by African American lesbian poet and activist Pat Parker, his recurring line was "where will you be when they come?"

This orientation toward movement activism was not simply an element of BWMT's national gatherings. It also shows up at the local level, as the newsletters of many chapters reveal. One service that these newsletters performed was to keep members informed about current issues. At a time when the mainstream media's coverage of LGBTQ news was still sparse and sporadic and thus easy to miss, BWMT newsletters often reprinted articles that had appeared in the local press as well as in national outlets. And, of course, chapters engaged in local organizing. Philadelphia, for instance, undertook a "Bar Discrimination Project" and issued a report on it. BWMT also used its national conventions to give a boost to local organizing against racism in the LGBTQ community. Gathering in a different city each year and scheduling the convention to coincide with Pride Week and the annual Pride March, BWMT guaranteed that a very large interracial contingent would march in the parade.

A prominent feature of the newsletters from 1987 was the avid recruitment and encouragement of readers to come to the 1987 March on Washington. New York's newsletter announced to its members, "Of course you're coming . . . to Washington!" Louisville provided its members with forms to reserve a seat on the buses that had been rented to take local folks to the nation's capital. And after the march, newsletters reported extensively on the event, highlighting the turn-out of five hundred thousand. The Memphis newsletter contained a report from a member who had also attended the earlier 1979 March on Washington. He noted that, eight years later, there was "a harder edge, a more profound, deeper frustration and urgency to our demands, our wants, and our needs . . . Our voices were more strident this time; our anger deeper; our will to resist stronger."

A document that particularly caught my attention and that serves as powerful evidence of the activist intentions of BWMT's leadership was a 150-page publication, *Resisting Racism: An Action Guide*. It included outlines and resource materials for twenty different workshops intended to equip participants with tools and knowledge to counter racism. Workshops included "Confronting Racism in the Gay/Lesbian Community"; "Bar Discrimination," the issue that had helped to bring BWMT into existence; and "Addressing Racism in Lesbian and Gay Organizations." The action guide reprinted resource tools for developing action plans to resist racism and for addressing racism and homophobia in the media. There was material from lesbian-of-color writers like Audre Lorde and Cherrie Moraga. There were articles titled "Racism in the Movement" and "What Black History Month Should Mean to White Gays."

Taken together, the work of Black and White Men Together at both the local and national level highlights the efforts made by some gay men in the 1980s and 1990s to challenge racism both within and beyond the gay male community in many cities across the US.

28

Chicago Mobilizes to March on Washington

Chicago's history has never been self-contained. It does not exist in a silo protected from the world around it. Whether it is the influence of a Jane Addams or a Barack Obama, the work of Chicago's residents has reached beyond the boundaries of the city and the state of Illinois. Similarly, events in Chicago can have a far-reaching impact. The conference "Sexual Orientation and the Law" helped strengthen a national network of legal activists. And, at the same time, events with a national scope can reach into Chicago and have a deep effect on the local. The 1987 national March on Washington offers such an example.

The importance of the 1987 March on Washington cannot be overstated. It put the organized LGBTQ community on the national stage as never before. There had been a first lesbian and gay national march in 1979, but it drew fewer than one hundred thousand people to Washington. By the standards of the time, that marked it as decidedly unimpressive. By 1987, just eight years later, much had changed. The AIDS epidemic was raging across America, killing men who had sex with men in staggering numbers. The Reagan administration was disgracefully ignoring it. The president did not even mention AIDS for the first five years of the epidemic, even as the caseload and deaths reached the tens of thousands. In 1986, in

The research for this essay is based on the 1987 March on Washington Collection, Gerber/Hart Library and Archives.

Bowers v. Hardwick, the Supreme Court added to the fury by uphold-
ing the constitutionality of state sodomy laws, with language that
was gratuitously contemptuous of same-sex love and relationships.
Put all this together, and the result was a march of five hundred
thousand people in October 1987, perhaps the largest protest march
to ever assemble in the nation's capital.

But there was more. There was also mass civil disobedience and
arrests in front of the Supreme Court; a mass wedding of same-sex
couples to protest the absence of family recognition; the powerful display, for the first time, of the Names Project Memorial Quilt
on the Washington Mall; a national gathering of bisexual activists;
and a meeting of AIDS activists from across the United States. Key
speakers at the rally were the Reverend Jesse Jackson, longtime African American civil rights leader and a candidate in 1984 for the
Democratic presidential nomination; Cesar Chavez, head of the
United Farmworkers Union and perhaps the most visible Chicano
leader in the US; and Eleanor Smeal, president of the National Organization for Women, the largest feminist organization in the United
States. Their participation was a dramatic sign that the lesbian and
gay rights movement of those years had come of age and was recognized as a component of the broad struggle for social and economic
justice in the United States.

Documents in the papers of Chicago's March on Washington
chapter provide a glimpse into just how wide and deep the organizing for the march was. The national steering committee had
representatives from eighteen states and from fifteen national organizations, and there were local committees in forty-three states.
For instance, three cities in Alabama, six in Georgia, eight in North
Carolina, and three in Maine had an organizing structure to get
people to Washington. A list of endorsers of the march filled several pages. It included labor unions, religious groups, and women's
organizations, as well as national, state, and local elected officials.
Each one of those endorsements came because an activist reached
out to key figures in those groups, talked about the march and the

issues, and persuaded them to lobby within their organization for an endorsement.

March organizers planned a number of events that involved civil disobedience. A condition of joining in the civil disobedience outside the Supreme Court was that participants belong to a local affinity group. This meant that, in the summer and early fall of 1987, deep and trusting relationships were forming among groups of activists in cities across the country. The Chicago committee was one of many that held training sessions in advance. How much, I found myself wondering, did this contribute to the explosion of local direct-action protests by ACT UP and other AIDS activist groups in the months and years after the March on Washington, both in Chicago and around the country. With so many activists being trained in the art of civil disobedience, how could it not continue at home after the march was over? Moreover, the Chicago committee as well as local organizing committees elsewhere engaged in special fundraising and outreach efforts to make sure that significant numbers of people with AIDS (PWAs) were able to participate in the march. Thus, the fight against AIDS was an essential part of the March on Washington, and the march also contributed importantly to moving that fight forward.

The effort to get people to Washington and to ensure that the march was a resounding success moved activism forward in Chicago as well. Julie Valloni and Victor Salvo were the cochairs of the committee. In the course of organizing Chicagoans to go to Washington, they and other committee members sought local endorsements, a process that undoubtedly built support for a city nondiscrimination ordinance, which still had not passed in 1987. They also worked closely with media in Chicago. One result was front-page coverage of the march by the *Chicago Sun-Times*. Perhaps the most visible local achievement was the endorsement letter the committee received from Mayor Harold Washington, the city's first African American mayor and a progressive ally of the LGBTQ community. "It is with enthusiasm that I endorse the National March on Washington for Lesbian and Gay Rights," he wrote in his letter of September 17. "The breadth of the issues highlighted by the March—against racism and apartheid, as well as for civil rights—is consistent with the historic thrust of struggles for civil rights in this country." The mayor also issued a proclamation pronouncing October 11, 1987, as "Chicago March on Washington for Lesbian and Gay Rights Day." Working hard to get a civil rights ordinance passed in Chicago, Mayor Washington also wrote, "The March will in turn support passage of a comprehensive Human Rights Ordinance here in Chicago." Such a law was finally enacted a year after the March on Washington.

While the work of organizing a national march can seem like a somber, stressful effort, the list of groups supporting the march included one that must have provoked laughter from everyone who encountered it. Soon after the *Hardwick* decision and at the height of the AIDS epidemic, the Vatican issued in October 1986 a major document on homosexuality that provoked a great deal of criticism and outrage, since it supported a theology that defined homosexual behavior as criminal. But one result was that, in Chicago, it led to the formation of a new group called POPE. The acronym stood for Pissed-Off Pansies Energized, and its members used that energy to help get Chicagoans to Washington. The group serves as a useful reminder that a sense of humor is often to be found embedded in the serious work of social justice activism. Indeed, humor may very well be an essential feature of successful activist endeavors.

29

Confronting AIDS: The Response of Black and White Men Together

LGBTQ life and activism in the 1980s and 1990s cannot be separated from the onslaught of AIDS. The epidemic was responsible for the large turnout at the March on Washington. It also helped reshape the work of many existing organizations. Such was the case with Black and White Men Together.

The first decade of Black and White Men Together coincided with the onset of the AIDS epidemic. The initial reports on AIDS appeared in June 1981, the same month that BWMT held its first annual conference. By 1988, over one hundred members of BWMT had passed away as a result of AIDS. In 1989, Michael J. Smith, the founder of the organization, died. By its tenth anniversary conference in 1990, the celebratory tone of the gathering was necessarily tempered by the explosion of AIDS cases. And the growth in the caseload did not subside. By mid-1996, there were 566,000 reported AIDS cases, 343,000 deaths, and a likely several hundred thousand more individuals who were HIV positive but whose condition was not known to health officials. African Americans were disproportionately affected. Though only 12 percent of the population, they accounted in 1996 for 38 percent of Americans known to be living with AIDS.

Reading through the many newsletters that local chapters pro-

The research for this essay is based on the Ken Allen Papers and the Wendell Reid Papers, Gerber/Hart Library and Archives.

duced makes it clear that AIDS was a major concern. "Minorities Are Hardest Hit by AIDS," an early issue of the Chicago chapter newsletter proclaimed. BWMT leaders spoke out forcefully about the need to take action. Board member Preston Shumaker penned a very powerful call to arms. "While masses of us are partying, AIDS continues to take its toll," he wrote. "We must become abreast of all the issues . . . Nobody is going to give us our rights; we must fight like hell for them!"

The response of many chapters to the epidemic was impressive. In August 1987, the Centers for Disease Control held the "AIDS in the USA Minority Communities" conference in Atlanta. Several BWMT members attended the conference, and when they returned home, the experience added a sense of urgency to their efforts at community education and political engagement. For instance, Tallahassee chapter members who went to the conference learned that Florida seemed to have an especially heavy concentration of black men with HIV. Soon after, members testified before their county commission in support of more funding for AIDS and sexually transmitted disease education. They also met with staff in the Florida state AIDS office to share what they learned at the conference, and they distributed materials on AIDS to elected officials. In an effort to keep its members informed, the Tallahassee chapter filled its newsletter in the months after the conference with reprints of articles on AIDS from major national newspapers.

The imperative to educate and to act emerges clearly in the source materials from 1987 and later. The 1987 March on Washington, which many BWMT members attended, had described itself in part as a "March against AIDS." Local chapters seem to have absorbed that message. For instance, like Tallahassee, the Louisville, Kentucky, chapter reprinted in its newsletter many articles on AIDS. It also lobbied the Department of Health Services to do more to educate the public about the epidemic and reported with satisfaction in 1987 that the department had expanded its AIDS education staff from one to three. The Memphis chapter reprinted a long essay by the Reverend Carl Bean, a gay African American minister in Los

Angeles who served the LGBTQ community. Confronted with the devastation that AIDS was wreaking on his congregation, Reverend Bean had formed a pioneering project to educate people about AIDS, serve those in need, and slow the spread of the disease. His article was an inspirational piece designed to motivate community members in other cities to do their part.

The tragedy of AIDS made even more imperative the dual mission of Black and White Men Together, to confront racism within the gay community and homophobia within the African American community. In the wake of the Centers for Disease Control conference in Atlanta, the Cincinnati chapter wrote a long editorial-style essay that it titled "AIDS, Homophobia, and Racism." It admitted that black organizations and leaders were "finally acknowledging the threat that AIDS poses to the black community." At the same time, it reported a tendency in the larger African American community to claim that "the majority of black PWAs are heterosexuals who got the syndrome from IV drug use." But, it went on, "this is far from the truth." Gay black men found themselves caught in the middle between the silences of white racism and the denials of black homophobia. "This combination of white media whiteout on black PWAs and a resulting black disinterest in preventive techniques because they didn't think AIDS was their concern together worked hand-in-hand to intensify the AIDS crisis." The contents of chapter newsletters indicate that BWMT members around the country were making it their mission to challenge these silences and the tragedy that such silence was producing.

As I mentioned in the Amigas Latinas essay, a phrase that I use to describe the AIDS crisis of the 1980s and its impact was "AIDS changes everything." One significant manifestation of this is the way, by the end of the decade, the epidemic was making government funding available for education, prevention, and health services projects. The Clinton administration accelerated this trend and secured an unprecedented level of resources to fight the epidemic. Dozens of community-based organizations across the United States were direct recipients of federal funds, and many more received federal funding indirectly through grants from state agencies. LGBTQ organizations were among the beneficiaries. Groups that had relied entirely on the labor of volunteers were now able to hire staff and, in the process, become more stable. Although the funding had AIDS prevention and care as its primary goal, organizations serving a community of men who have sex with men inevitably had an impact on the LGBTQ community more generally.

The story of Black and White Men Together confirms this perspective. Materials on the eighth annual convention held in Boston in 1988 report on BWMT's work in creating a National Task Force on AIDS Prevention. The task force received a federal grant of half a million dollars, which allowed it to hire seven staff members. Two years later, BWMT helped found the National Minority AIDS Council, which rapidly became a key player in the fight against AIDS. Locally, the Los Angeles chapter received a grant to do AIDS education work. In many other ways as well, AIDS pushed BWMT chapters into greater levels of public engagement. By the mid-1990s, for instance, the Chicago chapter had helped to create and was a major participant in an African American AIDS Walk through the predominantly black South Side. Its goal was not only to raise money for AIDS services but also to raise consciousness in the broader community about the need to take action and respond to the epidemic.

Of course, one wishes that the increased visibility of African American gay men and the dual fight against racism and homophobia might have happened without the horrific loss of life that came with the AIDS epidemic. Nonetheless, it is important to realize that, in Chicago and across the United States, BWMT chapters played an important role in organizing a vigorous response to the challenges that AIDS presented.

30
The Rise of Bisexual Activism

One of the pleasant surprises that comes from snooping through the collections at Gerber/Hart is seeing how rich with information even small collections can be. The papers of Melissa Ann Merry are a perfect illustration of that.

Merry was a Chicago-based bisexual activist and performer. Born in Canton, Ohio, in 1963, she went to college at Eastern Michigan University and then moved to Chicago soon after graduating in 1986. It was in Chicago that she came out as bisexual, and she quickly plunged into a world of bisexual activism that was coming together in the late 1980s and early 1990s. Locally, she got involved in the Bisexual Action Coalition (BIPAC) and was also a Midwest representative to the national organization BiNet (Bisexual Action Network of the USA), which grew out of the first national bisexual conference, held in San Francisco in June 1990. Fortunately for those interested in the bisexual movement of these years, Merry saved newsletters and clipped articles from magazines and newspapers. Thus, her papers can teach us about more than her own individual activism; they offer a view of the broad reach of bisexual organizing from the late 1980s to the mid-1990s.

For me, the clearest thing that emerges from Merry's experience is that the years from 1987 to 1994 were critically important in the

Research for this essay is based on the Melissa Ann Merry Papers, Gerber/Hart Library and Archives.

building of a visible bisexual presence in what, until then, had been referred to as the "gay and lesbian" movement. At least a couple of things seem to account for the shift, one negative and one positive. The negative factor was the AIDS epidemic and how it was portrayed. The alarmist style of writing about AIDS in the mid-1980s often focused on the threat that this "gay" disease might pose to the so-called general population, a phrase that the mainstream media used frequently. In this imaginary, bisexuals were seen as the transmitters of this killer virus from the gay male world to everyone else. This blame-the-bisexual narrative (even though the word "bisexual" was rarely used) was a powerful motivator for organizing in order to be able to counter it effectively.

The positive factor was the series of national marches that occurred in the space of seven years: the 1987 and 1993 Marches on Washington and the 1994 Stonewall 25 commemoration in New York City. The 1987 March on Washington brought half a million people together, and among the marchers was a bisexual contingent. Many members of the contingent met together that weekend to discuss future possibilities, a gathering that one magazine article described as "the first nationwide bisexual gathering in the U.S." Three years later, in June 1990, bisexuals convened in San Francisco for a conference that brought five hundred activists together. Ongoing discussions led to the formation the following year of BiNet, a national organization that linked local activists together. By the summer of 1992, according to an *Advocate* article that Merry saved, there were over 250 organizations of bisexuals in the United States.

With this kind of groundwork, bisexuals were in a strong position to advocate for formal inclusion in the 1993 March on Washington. The existence of so many organizations around the country meant that bisexual activists were able to argue their case with and put pressure on many of the local representatives serving on the national organizing committee so that the decision was made in 1992 to name the event a march for "Lesbian, Gay, and Bi Equal Rights." Once that was achieved, planning for the march provided a great spur to local organizing across the US to make sure, not only that bisexuals participated in the march, but also that the turnout was large. BiNet leaders also planned a national conference for that same weekend in Washington. Thus, the April 1993 March on Washington proved to be not a single event, but a tool that had consequences both before and after in the heightened level of local organization that it produced. The same can be said of the buildup for and aftermath of Stonewall 25, which brought massive numbers of people to New York in June 1994 and achieved extraordinary media visibility. Bisexuals used the event not only as an opportunity to be a visible contingent in the mass march that occurred, but also to hold an international bisexual conference in New York that weekend.

All three of these marches led both to more local organizing and to higher levels of national networking, which showed itself in a number of ways. For one, an increasing number of campus groups began to explicitly include bisexuals in their names and in their organized activities. In many movement settings and community events, the term "lesbigay" was increasingly substituted for "lesbian and gay." And, perhaps most impressively, the increasing breadth and depth of bisexual organizing can be seen in the substantial number of bisexual-focused publications from the early and mid-1990s. Among the newsletters that Merry saved are *Anything That Moves*, from the San Francisco Bay Area; *Bi-Lines*, from Madison, Wisconsin; *Bi-Monthly*, from Champaign-Urbana, Illinois; *Boston Bisexual Women's Network Newsletter*; *North by Northwest*, out of Seattle; *Bi-Atlanta*; *Bi-Centrist*, from Washington, DC; *Bi-Lines*, from Chicago; and *Bi-Focus* from Philadelphia. The fact that activists were producing so many publications in the early 1990s suggests that there are many stories about bisexual organizing still waiting to be told.

These newsletters and community magazines make it clear that bisexuals were organizing on a far more extensive scale during this period than is commonly recognized in current histories of the LGBTQ movement. In rare instances, an individual might prove capable of writing, producing, and distributing such a publication. But, more typically, it requires a group to do the work of gathering the information, writing it up, and building an audience to read the material and sustain the newsletter or magazine. The existence of publications like these also suggests that there were sufficient groups, issues, and campaigns to write about, thereby confirming that this was a period of intense and productive bisexual activism.

Finally, history is reconstructed not just through the words that people from the past left behind, but also from material objects that they produced. As part of their organizing work, bisexual activists created T-shirts, buttons, and political stickers to increase their visibility and spread a political message. Many of them display a sense of humor that will easily produce chortles of laughter for the knowing, but may also perhaps produce a moment of shock that successfully grabs the attention of those who may never have thought of bisexuality before. To mention just a few that Melissa Ann Merry saved for posterity: there is a T-shirt that reads "Caution: Ice-pick wielding bisexual fag-dyke. Do not agitate!" Another portrays a line of women, some front-to-back, others face-to-face, with looks of ecstasy on their faces and the words "Primal Clit: Lesbians and Bi-Womyn in Radical Action." There were stickers, meant to be placed on poles and walls and cars, one of which read "Bisexuals Don't Sit on Fences. We Build Bridges!!!" And finally, Merry had a trove of buttons, among them the following: "I'm Bisexual—You're Confused"; "Bi-Sexuals Are Equal Opportunity Lovers"; and "Two Roads Diverged in a Yellow Wood . . . and I Took Both."

Although Melissa Ann Merry immersed herself in an activist world for only a limited number of years, the material she collected in the course of her work allows for rich insight into a key stretch of bisexual activism in the United States.

31

Impact '88: Becoming a Force in Electoral Politics

When Gary Nepon ran for public office in 1978 as an openly gay political candidate in Chicago, the LGBTQ community still existed on the margins of the city's politics. But a mere decade later, changes of consequence were percolating through the political system. Evidence of the change can be found in the work of Carole Powell.

Powell was a longtime activist from the South. She had worked with national women's organizations, had organized major voter registration drives in Tennessee, and had been involved with lesbian and gay activism when this was still uncommon in the region. Relocating to Chicago in the 1980s, she was hired in 1988 to coordinate "Lesbian and Gay Voter Impact '88," a massive effort to register voters and thus demonstrate the political power of the community. Building on the energy that the AIDS epidemic was arousing and the March on Washington had intensified, the drive was a cooperative effort of two preexisting organizations. Impact: Chicago's Gay and Lesbian Political Action Committee was a nonpartisan organization that endorsed candidates based on their support for community issues. The Lesbian and Gay Progressive Democratic Organization was a left-of-center activist group working both within the Democratic Party and in the broader community for change. LGPDO included many of the city's most visible activists—figures

Research for this essay is based on the Carole Powell Papers, Gerber/Hart Library and Archives.

such as Ron Sable, an activist doctor who had been deeply involved with the Howard Brown Clinic, which provided medical services to the LGBTQ community, and who had run for the city's board of alderman; Art Johnston, owner of Sidetrack, a very popular bar on Halsted Street; Patricia Logue, who would later head Lambda Legal's Midwest Office in Chicago; and Victor Salvo and Julie Vallone, who had coordinated Chicago's 1987 March on Washington committee. At the kickoff dinner for Impact in the winter of 1988, keynote speakers included Pat Norman, who had been a national cochair of the enormously successful March on Washington the previous year, and Congressman Barney Frank from Massachusetts, who had recently come out.

Voter registration can be a deeply boring and frustrating experience. One walks a neighborhood or knocks on doors hoping that people will be responsive and interrupt their day to fill out forms so that they can do something that they have not bothered to do before. Or you attend public events where crowds are gathered and people are enjoying themselves, and, instead of having fun with them, you distract them from the fun they were having. Yet this didn't stop Powell and her group of organizers from pressing forward. They trained 150 volunteers to register voters, and they set for themselves a goal of ten to fifteen thousand new voters. From Pride Week in late June, when the campaign was launched with a press conference outside City Hall, until October 11, the last day that one could register and be entitled to vote in the 1988 elections, Impact '88 was out on the streets of Chicago.

The voter registration drive maintained an extremely high level of visibility. As Powell described it in a report on the campaign, "any and every event that we were aware of in the lesbian and gay community was attended." The city's gay bars proved "extremely cooperative . . . every gay business approached assisted us in some way." Its calendar of activities had registrars scheduled to stand outside supermarkets and to attend every gay and lesbian sporting event for weeks. A particularly important moment came during July, when the Names Project AIDS Memorial Quilt was displayed for the first time in Chicago at Navy Pier. As Chicagoans came face-to-face with this powerful reminder of the lives lost to an epidemic fueled by homophobia, Impact '88 volunteers were there to register new voters. Their efforts proved, in Powell's words, "extremely successful."

Reflecting the influence of the large contingent of left-wing progressives on its steering committee, Impact '88 reached out to a broad range of coalition partners. "A number of individuals from the black and Hispanic communities did contribute substantially," Powell wrote in her evaluation of the drive. "A great many of the voters registered came from these communities." Feminist organizations, such as Planned Parenthood, the National Abortion Rights Action League, and the National Organization for Women, also cooperated.

By almost any standard of measurement, Impact '88 succeeded. By the end of the registration season in October, the number of new voters it had added to the rolls—17,225—exceeded its most optimistic goals. While the campaign was underway, it received coverage from both the *Chicago Tribune* and the *Chicago Sun-Times*, so that politicians of every stripe had to be aware of it. Chicago was preparing that fall for a mayoral primary and election to be held in February and April of 1989, and every major candidate came out in favor of legislation to prohibit discrimination based on sexual orientation. And, in December 1988, two months after the end of Impact's voter registration campaign, the city council did in fact pass such legislation, by an impressive margin of 28–17.

While it would be hard to prove definitively that Impact '88 was the key factor in this major legislative success, its role seems undeniable. When the campaign started in the summer, Chicago and Illinois did not have an admirable record on LGBTQ issues. "The Illinois legislature has enacted the worst AIDS-related legislation anywhere in the U.S.," one of Impact's letters to its supporters declared. Just two years earlier, in 1986, the Chicago City Council had decisively rejected a sexual orientation antidiscrimination bill, 30–18. Joseph Bernardin, Chicago's Roman Catholic archbishop, had been outspoken in his opposition to it. His stance had not changed in the intervening two years, but the vote of many city council members had shifted. Surely a highly visible, well-organized, and extremely successful voter registration drive must have contributed to this signal legislative victory. Impact '88 described it as "a true acknowledgment of our strength."

Social movements are, by definition, collective efforts. They depend on significant numbers of people acting together for a common cause. But the collective is always composed of individuals. In the case of Impact '88, one individual especially stands out, Norman Sloan. He single-handedly registered over six thousand new voters, more than a third of the total. Such a total suggests that he was out on the streets, every day, tracking down possible registrants. The numbers he accumulated serve as a powerful reminder that individuals can make a difference in history.

32
Facing Off with the Media:
The Work of GLAAD-Chicago

On more than a few occasions in the last several years, as I have read the *New York Times* or the *Chicago Tribune* in the morning, I have had the sensation that I was reading an LGBTQ community newspaper. The range and number of stories have sometimes been staggering. For a long stretch, there were articles on the fight for marriage equality. More recently, transgender issues have figured prominently. But I was also encountering news about a broad swath of topics, including changes in federal policies, tech industry initiatives, sports figures coming out, arts and culture profiles, young people organizing in their schools, op-ed pieces, and much, much more. In addition to the quantity of material, the positive perspective embedded in the reporting has also been noteworthy. The underlying point of view in the coverage and reporting has been one that affirms and validates LGBTQ communities and their fight for acceptance and justice. The fact that such coverage came in such different newspapers—the liberal *New York Times* and the conservative, Republican-oriented *Chicago Tribune*—suggests how deeply and widely LGBTQ people and issues are being incorporated into mainstream society.

While much more change still needs to happen, this is a far cry from the situation fifty years ago. In the pre-Stonewall years, before the rise of a militant movement, the media's response toward the

Research for this essay is based on the records of GLAAD-Chicago, Gerber/Hart Library and Archives.

community more typically alternated between a deep silence—no mention or recognition at all—and lurid stories that emphasized crime, danger, and moral corruption. This did not all magically change after Stonewall and the rise of a gay liberation movement. Part of what contributed to the rapid spread of AIDS in the 1980s was the tendency of the media either to ignore the story, thus perpetuating ignorance and an inability to act effectively against its spread, or to sensationalize the epidemic and thus perpetuate the deep cultural and institutional bias against men who have sex with men.

The slowness of the media to change comes through very clearly in the work of GLAAD-Chicago. GLAAD, which stands for Gay and Lesbian Alliance against Defamation, was a media watchdog organization formed in New York City in 1985 by Vito Russo and Darrell Yates Rist, both writers and activists, as well as others. They acted in response to some of the horrifying coverage of AIDS coming from papers like the *New York Post*, owned by the right-wing media mogul Rupert Murdoch. By the early 1990s, GLAAD had spawned perhaps a dozen local chapters, of which Chicago was one.

One of the major emphases in the work of GLAAD was its monitoring of the newly powerful "religious right," whose influence was growing during the Reagan presidency. GLAAD kept track of and collected publications produced by organizations like the Traditional Values Coalition, the Family Research Institute, Focus on the Family, and, locally, the Illinois Family Institute that, even in 2016, was still out there rousing opposition to initiatives designed to protect the safety and well-being of transgender youth. The work of Paul Cameron especially drew GLAAD's attention. A psychologist who was expelled from the American Psychological Association in 1983, Cameron founded the Institute for the Scientific Investigation of Sexuality (ironically, its initials are ISIS). He produced reports with titles like "Criminality, Social Disruption, and Homosexuality," "Child Molestation and Homosexuality," and "Murder, Violence, and Homosexuality." Among his claims was the wild and baseless assertion that homosexuals killed at least 68 percent of the victims of mass murders, an early example of what might be called "fake news." In the 1990s, organizations like the National Gay and Lesbian Task Force and People for the American Way were documenting the activities and media strategies of conservative religious activists, and the reports they issued were a valuable resource that GLAAD made use of in its work.

Interestingly, the work of a media watchdog group like GLAAD in these years was not confined to exposing extremists. Mainstream media outlets needed to be targeted as well. A 1994 study by GLAAD of the *Chicago Tribune* and the *Sun-Times* found "alarming developments with regard to recent coverage of gay and lesbian issues." Articles in the *Sun-Times*, the city's liberal daily paper, especially shocked GLAAD staffers in Chicago. In the space of two months in 1994, the paper published two editorials that sounded as if the editorial board had lifted passages directly out of a religious right report. In response to the suburb of Oak Park extending medical benefits to the same-sex partners of town employees, the *Sun-Times* editorialized about "the importance of more traditional families" and "the central role in society traditional families must still assume." Then, in an editorial coinciding with the twenty-fifth anniversary celebrations of the Stonewall Rebellion of 1969, the *Sun-Times* declared: "we oppose extending favored status to gays . . . the heterosexual majority is justifiably concerned that its values not be marginalized . . . and that a new set of rights not be extended to a privileged class." GLAAD's response was uncensored: "you have bought into the Religious Right's lies and myths," it wrote to the editorial page editor. The paper's claims, it said, were "vague and fallacious." The *Sun-Times*'s language was "frighteningly close to the phrases and code words used by Religious Right zealots." GLAAD's pressure led to a meeting between it and the *Sun-Times* editorial board.

GLAAD activists also documented some jaw-dropping examples of homophobia among individual mainstream journalists. Mike Royko was a Pulitzer Prize–winning columnist who was a fixture of the Chicago press for decades. He had a take-no-prisoners style of writing that called out politicians and other public figures. His biography of Mayor Daley, *Boss*, was a best seller. GLAAD received an anonymous unsigned memo, dated May 22, 1995, and with it a copy of a police report, dated December 17, 1994, documenting Royko's arrest on DUI and resisting arrest charges in conjunction with a car crash. The memo called attention to comments made by Royko that were contained in the report. Among other things, he screamed at the responding officer "you cocksucker" and "get your hands off me, you fucking fag." Later he yelled "get away from me. What are you, fags?" and "Jag off, queer," and finally, "What's your ethnicity, you fag?" Because of Royko's stature, the memo and report, which was sent to several LGBTQ organizations, created a media moment in Chicago. It also suggests how deeply embedded homophobia was in white male heterosexual culture.

GLAAD's work helps explain why the tone and content of media coverage of LGBTQ issues is different today than it was less than three decades ago. It did not happen by magic, by some mysterious process of evolution that brings progress. It took activist commitment and energy, a willingness to fight back and challenge media power brokers. As its records reveal, GLAAD-Chicago had an impact, and it is likely that other GLAAD chapters scattered across the United States also played a role in reshaping the media's stance toward the LGBTQ community.

33

Building Community: Peg Grey and the Power of Sports

As one of the few living Americans who has never watched a minute of a Super Bowl game, I may not be the best candidate to write an essay on the place of sports in LGBTQ life. But just as my lack of deep engagement in the world of music did not prevent me from recognizing the important role of a group like the Artemis Singers in building and sustaining lesbian community in Chicago, so too my distance from the world of athletics does not keep my historian's mind from grasping the significance of sports as a vehicle for strengthening community bonds. Two collections at Gerber/Hart speak to the power of sports, especially since the 1980s, as a tool for fashioning community ties and achieving goals beyond winning a game or a race. Frontrunners was a recreational organization that sponsored a host of activities, while Peg Grey was a passionate advocate for sports and participated in a wide variety of sporting activities and organizations.

Frontrunners had its beginnings in 1974 in San Francisco as the Lavender U Joggers. In 1978, the group changed its name to one taken from one of the most popular gay-themed novels of the decade, *The Frontrunner*, by Patricia Nell Warren, which tells the story of a track coach and the runner he falls in love with. As an organization, Frontrunners finally began to take off in 1981 when Tom

Research for this essay is based on the Peg Grey Papers and the records of Frontrunners/Frontwalkers, Gerber/Hart Library and Archives.

Waddell, an athlete from the 1968 Olympics who later came out as gay, decided to organize in San Francisco for the following year what he initially called the "Gay Olympic Games." In order to give the event more visibility, he arranged that, as with the Olympics, a torch would be carried by runners, in this case along a route through the United States. Thus, the approach of the games became a vehicle that, over a period of months, highlighted an image of LGBTQ runners. Suddenly the number of Frontrunner chapters began to multiply. The success of the games that summer and Waddell's promise that they would be held every four years also provided an impetus for an explosion of organized LGBTQ sports activity more broadly.

From the start, Peg Grey was a force for bringing organized sports activities to Chicago's LGBTQ community. Throughout 1981 she had been trying, without much success, to organize a gay and lesbian running club in Chicago. When she learned about the Gay Olympics and the opportunity to carry the torch through Chicago, it provided the handle she needed to form a Frontrunners club in the city. As its first public event, it almost immediately organized a Proud to Run race scheduled for early in the morning of Pride Sunday, before the big annual march occurred.

Initially, Frontrunners Chicago was primarily social in emphasis. Most of its members saw it as an alternative to the bar scene, a way to socialize with other gays (the membership was overwhelmingly male in its early years) without the intense cruising for sex, the excessive drinking, and the loud noise associated with nightlife in what was coming to be called "Boystown." Frontrunners sponsored weekly noncompetitive runs, with the opportunity to gather afterward for a meal. Sometimes groups of members signed up for one of the many races held throughout the city and suburbs in the course of a year. Frontrunner chapters were in communication with each other, and members from several cities occasionally traveled to participate in a run together, thus creating a large, visible contingent of gay and lesbian runners and developing wider social networks based on this common interest.

The Frontrunners newsletter provides fascinating glimpses

into the unintended consequences that participation in this athletic recreational community might have. In 1983, some members of the board of directors, including Peg Grey, suggested that, after holding its Proud to Run race in the early morning, Frontrunners should march as a contingent in the 1983 Pride Parade. The proposal aroused some very intense passions and revealed the prejudices that some of its members had. Several objected strongly to the idea. According to one account in the newsletter, "those opposed to Frontrunners['] participation felt that the parade shows the aspects of our lifestyle to be least proud of such as drag queens and the bar/bath scene." But a majority of members ultimately voted to march on Pride Sunday, and for at least one member, it proved to be a profound experience. As Dave Irvin described its impact on him:

> I had always been one of the people who criticized the parade and
> called it a circus. I was wrong. My closet door is not only open but off
> its hinges. My understanding of what it means to be proud has come
> full face. The feeling that I experienced as I walked down Broadway
> and especially while I helped carry the banner was overwhelming. I
> held my head high, yelled, laughed and was very proud to be a part of a
> great happening. It was truly a dawning, especially for me personally.

Soon, Frontrunners was doing more than simply sponsoring an annual race. Proud to Run became a fund-raising mechanism by which participants solicited from their friendship networks pledges of money that Frontrunners then donated to community-based service organizations. Members also signed up for other Chicago races, like the annual marathon and half marathon, where they wore Frontrunner T-shirts and solicited pledges to help fund LGBTQ-community projects. In 1986, members who ran in the marathon raised more than $15,000 that was then donated to Chicago House, an organization founded to provide living quarters to people with AIDS who were facing homelessness. Jump ahead two decades to 2006, and the Frontrunners' newsletter reported that, just in the previous twelve years, Proud to Run had raised nearly $250,000 for local organizations. In 2006, 690 runners participated. And the recipients extended beyond AIDS-related groups to a wide range of LGBTQ community organizations. Among its many beneficiaries was the Gerber/Hart Library and Archives.

As the reference to Chicago House suggests, AIDS figured in this deepening community involvement. The Chicago newsletter began referencing AIDS as early as 1983. It explicitly identified AIDS services as the reason for coordinated fund-raising efforts. The newsletter also served to educate members about the increasing threat of AIDS. Its May 1984 newsletter, for instance, reprinted an article from a publication of the Howard Brown Memorial Clinic, the main LGBTQ health-service organization in Chicago. "It appears that the AIDS problem is finally hitting home," the article announced. "We are seeing a real increase in the number of cases being reported in Chicago . . . We unfortunately cannot anticipate a downturn in the number of cases . . . AIDS can no longer be viewed as a bi-coastal phenomenon."

During the 1980s and 1990s, Peg Grey was perhaps more involved than any single individual not only in Frontrunners but in the rapidly growing world of organized LGBTQ athletics in Chicago. She served on the board of directors not only of Frontrunners but also of the larger Metropolitan Sports Association, the umbrella organization for LGBTQ sports. She was the force behind the decision to make Proud to Run an annual fund-raiser. She also worked with the Gay Games as a Chicago representative and pushed for the annual Race against AIDS, which became a valuable mechanism for raising funds to help people with AIDS.

Grey's papers are important for more than providing a profile of one of the key figures in the LGBTQ sports world in these decades. They also bring to the surface an issue that does not emerge from the Frontrunners papers—the issue of gender. Despite congressional passage in 1972 of Title IX, which prohibited discrimination based on sex in any programs or activities of educational institutions that received federal funding, and despite the high visibility of women's college basketball, athletics still carried the heavy connotation of "male." And Frontrunners reflected this. A very large majority of its members were male, and for years Grey was the only woman on its board of directors.

Grey did not leave behind a written trail of commentary on the obvious gender bias that existed in Frontrunners. But, after a decade of involvement with Frontrunners and the Metropolitan Sports Association, Grey decided to take action. In May 1991, she and a few others founded the Women's Sports Association. The WSA began with twenty members and organized softball games. Just three years later, it had three hundred members. It was sponsoring not only a softball league with nine teams, but also organized golf tournaments, tennis games, a volleyball league, and racquetball. Grey and others posted flyers publicizing the WSA in bars, bookstores, and restaurants in neighborhoods like Lakeview and Andersonville, where lesbians were known to socialize. And it soon began engaging its members with issues besides sports. It organized a health and wellness seminar in cooperation with the Lesbian Community Cancer Project and the Howard Brown Clinic; it organized fund-raisers for the LCCP; and it marched as a contingent in the annual Pride Parade. In important ways, sports became a mechanism for strengthening not only social bonds among lesbians in Chicago, but also for providing resources to support a range of other lesbian community projects.

34

Fighting the Military Ban: James Darby and the Effort to Mobilize Veterans

The first half of 1993 was a milestone moment for the LGBTQ movement in the United States. For more than six months, national political leaders fought over, and national and local media covered, an LGBTQ issue in the form of what was described by the phrase "gays in the military." As a presidential candidate the previous year, Democrat Bill Clinton had openly sought the support of lesbian and gay voters. He promised that, if elected, he would lift the ban on gays, lesbians, and bisexuals serving in the military. No candidate of a major political party had taken such a stand before.

But the promise proved easier to make than to deliver. Even before he assumed office in January, a strong and vocal opposition surfaced. General Colin Powell, who chaired the Joint Chiefs of Staff, expressed his reservations, claiming it would have a debilitating effect on morale. Sam Nunn, a Democratic senator from Georgia and the chair of the Senate's Armed Services Committee, was open in his disapproval and announced he would hold public hearings. Faced with such hostility from Washington power brokers, Clinton began to waffle. After months of public debate and congressional hearings, "Don't Ask, Don't Tell" was adopted as a policy. In effect, it said that lesbian, gay, and bisexual individuals could serve in the military, but only if they remained completely closeted. Clinton

Research for this essay is based on the James C. Darby Papers, Gerber/Hart Library and Archives.

claimed it as a step forward, but for activists it was a confirmation of policies rooted in homophobia.

Despite the defeat, the visibility of the issue and the passion it unleashed pushed the LGBTQ movement forward in major ways. One measure is the size of the 1993 March for Lesbian, Gay, and Bi Equal Rights that was held in April in Washington, DC. Planning for it had begun before the election and before the military issue had exploded on the front page of the nation's newspapers, but the debate energized community members across the United States. Some estimates of the turnout approached one million—an unprecedented number for a protest event.

The gays-in-the-military issue also spurred organizing among a very particular, but far-flung and large, constituency. In the popular imagination, the debate over the military ban brought up images of younger men and women, from their late teens into their early thirties, who comprised the overwhelming majority of service members. But there was another segment, one that stretched across the entire adult population, for whom the issue was consequential— veterans. Some of these, of course, were men and women who were removed from the military as far back as World War II because of charges related to homosexuality. They numbered in the tens of thousands since, in the 1950s and 1960s, the military was discharging as many as two thousand service members every year. But there was also a much, much larger constituency of lesbian, gay, and bisexual veterans—those who had completed their terms of service and received honorable discharges. If these men and women were to come out in large numbers, it might transform the public perception of the military's policy and dramatically alter its assumptions about the larger queer community.

Miriam Ben-Shalom, a former army sergeant who had challenged the military ban, was a key figure in the initial effort to mobilize veterans. In May 1990, almost three years before the "gays in the military" debate exploded in American politics, she and a few others had gathered in DC where they formed the national Gay, Lesbian and Bisexual Veterans of America (GLBVA). Ben-Shalom served as chairperson. She ran the organization out of her home in Milwaukee and, beginning in 1991, produced and mailed a bimonthly newsletter, the *Forward Observer*. By the spring of 1992, with the presidential campaign still in primary season, twenty-seven chapters had formed. And while groups had coalesced in cities known for their large queer community, there were also chapters in places that were not commonly thought of as centers for LGBTQ activism—places like Duluth, Georgia; Richmond, Virginia; and Rochester, New York.

Chicago was one of the cities that formed a chapter, and the person who kept it moving was an activist named James Darby. Darby was the key figure in the Chicago chapter and immersed himself in the national organization as well. He brought enthusiasm, optimism, determination, boldness, and a seemingly inexhaustible supply of energy to the work of organizing veterans. He wrote, produced, and circulated a newsletter for the Chicago chapter. Tracing the story of the gays-in-the-military campaign through his work and writing offers a vivid sense of the powerful emotions that the issue evoked.

Darby began publishing his newsletter in June 1992 soon after the chapter had its first meeting. "We are off and flying," he proclaimed to his readers. Darby reported on the work of Ben-Shalom, Perry Watkins, Tracy Thorne, and the other "brave souls who are willing to come out and challenge the Department of Defense." As the presidential campaign heated up, Darby urged veterans not to "waste your vote . . . there is only one presidential candidate who has emphatically stated that he will end the ban." A Clinton victory, he asserted, "will be a personal victory for every gay and lesbian veteran out there."

Under Darby's leadership, the Chicago chapter engaged in more than reportage. The month after the chapter was founded, the group had a small contingent of six members who participated in Chicago's annual Pride Parade. "The sight of gay and lesbian veterans marching in uniform left some parade watchers stunned," he reported. In November, several chapter members "crashed" the annual Veterans Day ceremony that the American Legion held in

Daley Plaza, in the heart of downtown Chicago. "As four officers of the American Legion and four big name politicians marched . . . with their wreaths . . . I squeezed in with our pink triangle floral piece." While there was "a little bit of grumbling" from some of the veterans, afterward the GLBVA group was invited to participate next year. "Wow! What a surprise that was," Darby admitted.

Almost immediately after Clinton's election, the military issue exploded in the press, and Darby's thorough reporting on it in the local newsletter brings to life the intensity of the discussion. Already by December there was "an avalanche of material." The daily newspaper in Rockford, Illinois, which Darby described as "the bastion of conservatism," had five articles in six days, and that was before Congress had begun to investigate the issue. Mike Royko, a major columnist in Chicago, titled his piece "Gays Have No Place in This Man's Army" and went on to ravage the gay and lesbian movement. Darby regularly included pages of news clippings with the monthly newsletter to keep his readers informed. Much of it, he acknowledged, was "openly hostile" to dropping the ban. By January, Randall Terry, the right-wing leader of Operation Rescue, an antiabortion group, had launched a campaign against dropping the ban. Picking up on Reagan's phrasing of the war against drugs, Terry described his campaign as "Just Say No to Homosexuals in the Military" and planned rallies in almost one hundred cities.

The backlash made organizing to lift the ban all the more important, and Darby's newsletter covered the effort thoroughly. A national bus tour of veterans launched in early March, and it traveled through twenty-four states, with rallies in support of it in thirty-two cities, including Chicago. The contingent of veterans received a prominent place near the front of the April March on Washington; thirty chapters from around the United States had members participating. Locally, Darby organized meetings with Illinois' congressional representatives, so that veterans could share their stories of service. Mayor Daley issued a proclamation honoring gay, lesbian, and bisexual veterans on Armed Services Day in May, and at the Pride Parade in June, the contingent of Chicago veterans marched directly behind the mayor's car. That year's Pride event was the largest ever in Chicago, with participation estimated at 140,000. "The crowds along the route were wildly enthusiastic," Darby wrote in his newsletter, which he was now producing twice a month. And in July, GLBVA members from Chicago and around the country planned two more events in the nation's capital. They marched as a contingent in the annual Independence Day Parade in Washington, and on July 15, they gathered at the Lincoln Memorial as part of a National Mobilization against the Ban.

When the decision to adopt Don't Ask, Don't Tell as policy came down in July, Darby described it as "nothing more than repackaged discrimination . . . It is not a compromise; it is a sellout." For him, it was evidence that the campaign to repeal the ban had to keep going and that the mobilization of veterans needed to continue and to grow. "We need to prove our existence," he told his readers. In the succeeding years, Darby remained as committed as ever to the goal of eliminating the ban completely. Not only did he continue to publish his Chicago newsletter, but he became a key figure in the national organization as well. He attended all the national conventions and, in 1997, was elected president of GLBVA. Each year, the national organization sent letters to every member of Congress, as well as to the president and the secretary of defense, laying out their issues and the injustice of the ban on gays, lesbians, and bisexuals serving openly in the military.

Working my way through the mass of newsletters that Darby produced and taking in his unceasing efforts to bring down the military ban, I could not help but admire his militancy and determination. But, at the same time, I came away with a sense that mobilizing veterans was not an easy task. Even at its height, the Chicago chapter remained small, never amounting to more than a few dozen members. The contingents that came together at Chicago's Pride Parades and at the March on Washington were large enough to be noticed by observers, but not impressive when one considers the potential size of the constituency. And, after Don't Ask, Don't Tell went into effect, it became harder and harder to bring people together for protest actions. Reading between the lines of both the national and the local newsletter, I sensed that GLVBA functioned far more as a social network for most of the veterans who connected with it than as a political action group. And, in a way, I could understand that. These men and women had internalized the necessity of the closet in order to survive their years in the military and leave with honorable discharges. Many were of a generation for whom wearing the mask rather than coming out of the closet was the norm, and they were not prepared to change course at this stage of their lives. Realizing this makes the work of someone like Darby even more remarkable and impressive.

35

The Presidential Advisory Council on HIV/AIDS

"Gays in the military" was not the only LGBTQ-related headline-making issue during the Clinton presidency. The mid-to-late 1990s were also particularly critical years in the history of AIDS in the United States. On one hand, the impact of the epidemic was devastating. It had reached deep into and far across the nation. By 1996 there were 343,000 deaths from AIDS and 566,000 reported cases. And, as the Centers for Disease Control and Prevention often emphasized, there were likely hundreds of thousands of additional cases that remained undetected because the circumstances of many individuals kept them from seeking medical care. Gay men, of course, were vastly overrepresented in this caseload, but they were not the only group disproportionately affected. In 1994, African Americans accounted for 32 percent of the known cases of AIDS; two years later, the figure had risen to 38 percent. By 1998, African Americans accounted for over 40 percent of new cases, and African American women constituted 60 percent of new cases among females.

At the same time, these years also saw the earliest signs of good news in the history of the epidemic. Protease inhibitors, the first drugs that seemed to successfully limit the spread of HIV in those already infected, became available in 1995. The impact showed

Research for this essay is based on the AIDS Conference Records, Gerber/Hart Library and Archives.

quickly. Deaths from AIDS declined for the first time the following year. And significant federal funds were becoming available in the mid-1990s both to fight the spread of the disease and to provide care and services to those who had it.

Robert Fogel was a Chicagoan who served on the Presidential Advisory Council on HIV/AIDS. The papers he donated to Gerber/Hart documenting the work of the council suggest how deeply engaged it was in trying to shape policy in progressive directions. Council subcommittees studied prevention efforts, the funding needs of those engaged in the fight against AIDS, and the international dimensions of the epidemic. The council put special attention on the challenges faced by racial and ethnic populations, and it was in frequent communication with key figures in the Clinton administration. The work of the council allows one to gain a perspective on the AIDS epidemic as seen and discussed in the heart of the national government.

While the Clinton administration had badly disappointed LGBTQ activists because of its support for a "Don't Ask, Don't Tell" resolution of the military issue, it was simultaneously in the process of developing a much better stance toward AIDS. It was far more active in responding to the epidemic than either President Reagan, who callously ignored it, or President Bush, whose response was measured. Clinton succeeded in increasing the level of federal AIDS money during his first term in office. He fought hard to have Ryan White Care Act funding reauthorized, and appropriations rose substantially, as did federal discretionary spending under his watch. Large numbers of community-based organizations were receiving government money, which allowed them to provide vital services to those who were sick and to engage actively in prevention and educational efforts in local communities. The Americans with Disabilities Act, which was passed in 1990, included HIV-positive status as a condition for which individuals were protected from discrimination. Under Clinton, the Justice Department and the Equal Employment Opportunities Commission actively enforced the law, as many hundreds of cases of discrimination came to their attention. Clinton was the first president to put forward a national strategy for fighting the epidemic. He spoke forthrightly about the disproportionate impact that AIDS was having upon racial minorities. And he made himself and key administration leaders accessible to the members of the presidential AIDS council, who brought on-the-ground knowledge to the policy discussions about AIDS.

What stood out most dramatically to me as I read through the documents that Fogel had collected about the council's work during the Clinton presidency was the delicate line that the council and its committees had to walk. To have any impact, the council needed to maintain good working relationships with the White House and various cabinet departments. The reports it produced are overt in the praise they direct at the Clinton administration. The 1996 Executive Summary Progress Report described as "remarkable and laudable" the fact that Clinton had succeeded in raising federal spending on AIDS substantially, especially at a time when a new Republican majority in Congress was so hostile to many domestic programs. In a 1997 letter to Clinton, the council wrote that "you can be justly proud" of a whole series of achievements: "securing unprecedented funding for AIDS, establishing the Offices of AIDS Research and National AIDS Policy, convening the White House Conference on HIV/AIDS, developing the first-ever National AIDS Strategy and setting a goal of development within a decade of a vaccine to prevent AIDS." All of these, it continued, "have been major milestones in this fight."

At the same time, however, the council could be very direct in its criticism. In 1996, a Republican Congress passed the Personal Responsibility and Work Opportunity Reconciliation Act, more commonly referred to as "welfare reform." The law placed a variety of limitations on the ability of Americans to qualify for welfare assistance. In a letter to Clinton, the council expressed appreciation for the administration's resistance to some of the most "meanspirited, bigoted and punitive provisions . . . originally proposed by Congress." But, in the end, Clinton signed the bill, which the council described as posing "grave risks to many people living with HIV." The law, it wrote, "potentially undermines the nation's fight against

AIDS . . . by withholding medical care from important segments of the HIV-infected population." By placing so many new restrictions on who can receive government assistance, the measure "undermines the safety net for people with HIV by potentially withholding or reducing cash assistance and food stamps." Especially through the targeting of those convicted of drug use, a population disproportionately affected by AIDS, the law played into support for a hierarchy among those with HIV, with some being considered innocent victims and others being seen as guilty spreaders of the disease.

That division between the deserving and the undeserving also led the council to take issue with the restrictions that the Clinton administration supported on the federal funding of prevention materials and educational campaigns. It expressed "disappointment with the Administration's lack of action on some of our recommendations, particularly regarding some of the more politically charged aspects of prevention and discrimination where greater courage and leadership are required." In a 1997 letter to Donna Shalala, the secretary of health and human services, the council was more specific. It called for "the removal of existing restrictions on the content of CDC-supported HIV-prevention materials." It was extremely concerned about the prohibition on the use of federal funds to support needle exchange programs, which especially impacted African Americans. Instead, it called on Shalala to establish "accuracy and appropriateness for the target audience as the sole criteria for assessing" the value of prevention methods.

The Prevention Subcommittee of the council was particularly open in its identification of the administration's weaknesses. "Local prevention efforts," it wrote in 1997, "are more effective when their delivery meets the special needs of different populations." It then specifically mentioned "youth, women infected heterosexually who had little or no knowledge of their risk, young gay men of color at high risk for infection, [and] incarcerated populations." Current resources, it concluded, "are not sufficient for implementing all needed programs at the local level."

The pressure of the council seemed to have some effect. In the fall of 1998, Clinton addressed the increasingly unequal distribution of new AIDS cases. A press release from the White House announced that "President Clinton Declares HIV/AIDS in Racial and Ethnic Minority Communities to Be a 'Severe and Ongoing Health Care Crisis' and Unveils New Initiative." At a press conference, Clinton said that "we're here to send out a word loud and clear: AIDS is a particularly severe and ongoing crisis in the African American and Hispanic communities." He announced the allocation of an additional $156 million in federal funds to target those disparities. Almost a hundred community-based organizations were receiving direct funding from the CDC for prevention work.

For students of social movements that aimed to challenge the inequalities that government often produced and reinforced, the work of the Presidential Advisory Council can prove very instructive. They provide a sense of how individuals, many of whom thought of themselves as activists, learned to work "the system" to effect change. One can see their accomplishments—how they pushed and prodded the Clinton administration to do more. But one also has to acknowledge the way they came up against the barriers that party politics and public opinion imposed upon the efforts of social justice advocates.

36

A Community Fights AIDS: The Work of BEHIV

The work of a Presidential Advisory Council on HIV/AIDS can seem far removed from the daily life of a community and its needs. But what happens in Washington can make a big difference back home. The story of BEHIV brings this out clearly.

BEHIV—the acronym stands for Better Existence with HIV— was, in its own words, "a private, not-for-profit AIDS service organization . . . whose mission is to improve the lives of people with HIV and AIDS." By the end of the 1980s, Chicago's ACT UP chapter was bringing unprecedented public attention to the epidemic with its militant protests against the government's neglect of the issue. The number of diagnosed cases and their geographic spread had made it increasingly clear that communities almost everywhere needed to put attention on the epidemic. In Evanston, a suburb just north of Chicago, a group of community activists came together in 1989 to form BEHIV, in response to what it viewed as "the alarming growth of HIV in Evanston, Chicago's north side, and the northern suburbs." From the start, it hoped both to provide direct services to people who were living with HIV and to engage in broad-based community education efforts to prevent more people from being infected with the HIV retrovirus.

BEHIV quickly cast a wide net in terms of its outreach and services. By the early 1990s, it was conducting fifteen educational programs a

Research for this essay is based on the BEHIV Records, Gerber/Hart Library and Archives.

month, as it addressed schools, churches, community organizations, and professional groups, giving them basic information about AIDS and its prevention. It established a youth outreach center that offered a range of recreational and educational activities for teenagers, "a fun, safe place where kids can socialize, as well as learn about HIV." A majority of those participating were African American youth. Besides its educational efforts, over time it attracted more and more clients who were HIV positive or had developed full-blown AIDS. BEHIV provided them with a comprehensive set of services. It managed their cases; helped them find medical care; guided them through the process of applying for government assistance; investigated housing opportunities; distributed meals for people with HIV/AIDS in Chicago's northern suburbs; and offered substance abuse counseling. One of its more creative programs was its art therapy, where clients were encouraged to express their feelings through painting and drawing. The program proved so popular and attracted so much positive attention that BEHIV began arranging for exhibits of its clients' art in public spaces around Evanston and surrounding communities.

Although AIDS initially had the public image of a "gay disease," by the early 1990s there was more awareness of its impact on other populations. BEHIV was representative of that change. Though it certainly had gay male clients, it was not founded as a gay-identified organization, and its work reached beyond that population into communities—Evanston, Arlington Heights, the Rogers Park neighborhood of Chicago—with a diverse population. By 1995, its Rogers Park office was receiving two hundred drop-in clients a month, spread across a spectrum of racial, ethnic, and sexual identities as well as a wide range of ages. Two years later, the BEHIV newsletter explicitly acknowledged that "the face of AIDS has changed over the years." With support from Chicago's Department of Public Health, its Rogers Park team initiated "street outreach" services designed specifically to reach "sexually active men, primarily men of color."

BEHIV's growth in the course of the 1990s illustrates the connections between the local and the national. Not long after its founding, federal money to support AIDS service provision became available.

In 1990, Congress passed the Ryan White Care Act, the primary funding mechanism for a broad range of services to people with AIDS. That same year, it also authorized appropriations for Housing Opportunities for Persons with AIDS (HOPWA), a program that addressed the increasing homelessness of people with AIDS, who often found themselves unable to pay their rent because their illness left them unemployed. By 1993, a combination of federal and state funding, along with the support of local donors, allowed BEHIV to have a staff of nine in addition to its many community volunteers.

But, as the work of the Presidential Advisory Council on HIV/ AIDS strongly suggested, the Clinton administration's support for the fight against AIDS significantly expanded the amount of federal money that was available, and this had a dramatic impact on BEHIV. Its budget in 1997 had grown to well over a million dollars, and federal money accounted for 60 percent of its total revenues. Because of the increase in funding, its paid staff had almost tripled to twenty-four. The number of clients it served had increased tenfold from its first year of operation. Its workshops were reaching nine thousand individuals a year, and its educational materials circulated even more widely, reaching roughly seventy thousand people.

One of the more impressive aspects of BEHIV was the willingness of the organization to take on controversial issues, even with its dependence on federal money. The Presidential Advisory Council had criticized the Clinton administration for not pushing hard on the issue of needle exchange as a key measure for containing the spread of AIDS. Especially as its clientele came to include more African Americans, BEHIV confronted this issue directly by producing and distributing a pamphlet, *Why Do We Need Needle Exchange?* In its work with youth, who were a major constituency, it consistently emphasized the importance of safer sex practices, rather than engage in a state of denial about teenage sexual activity. One of its youth-oriented pamphlets, "HIV Is Everywhere. Believe It," forthrightly declared, "Always, always, always use a condom." In its outreach to suburban high schools, BEHIV not only offered workshops designed to educate teenagers about HIV/AIDS and methods of prevention.

It also actively recruited them into the work of community service and education. Young people answered phones and provided information to callers. They cleaned apartments for those who were suffering from the opportunistic infections that came with AIDS and, in the process, witnessed at close hand the ravages of HIV. And BEHIV put its teenage volunteers to work assembling "condom kits," which they then distributed in the community.

Although service and education were at the core of its mission, at times BEHIV also found itself having to venture into more overtly political activities. As Republican strength in Congress grew in the 1990s, and then under the Bush administration at the start of the new century, the prospect of cutbacks in government spending increased. BEHIV pushed its volunteers to call members of Congress and email their representatives to explain what federal appropriations under Ryan White and HOPWA were actually accomplishing. As its history makes clear, the divide between community service and political mobilization was not a hard-and-fast one.

BEHIV's work also makes the human cost of the epidemic immediate. Its newsletter frequently contained obituaries—not only of recipients of their services, but also of volunteers and members of its board of directors. BEHIV was not simply an organization that helped "others." Many of its core members were experiencing the epidemic directly, and it motivated them to go out into the world and make a difference.

Even as the toll of AIDS struck very close to home, BEHIV activists also preserved a sense of humor. In its prevention work, BEHIV sent volunteers onto the streets and into neighborhood businesses and institutions to distribute condom kits. Those going to gay bars labeled themselves "Condom Cops," consciously playing on the history of police raids. And those walking the streets of Evanston's African American neighborhood used the moniker "Rubber Brothers" to draw teenagers and young adults into discussions of safer sex and HIV prevention. The laughter this must have elicited in many encounters was undoubtedly a useful tool in opening the door to conversation and providing the beginnings of much-needed prevention education.

37
Making Schools Safe

For BEHIV, working with youth on issues of sexuality seemed like a natural part of its mission in the 1990s. But, back in the 1970s, when I first started doing research on pre-Stonewall activism, I can remember being struck by a notably different perspective. Organizational leaders repeatedly emphasized that membership and attendance at events were age restricted. If you had not reached adulthood, you did not have a place in this world of social and political activism.

The rationale behind this was not hard to figure out. Homosexuals were commonly portrayed as predators by nature, as corrupters of youth. In order not to feed this stereotype, the homophile activists of the pre-Stonewall era made sure that young people were kept outside this new and still small activist world. Of course, that decision came with a price. At a time when there was almost no positive information about or images of LGBTQ people in American culture, queer youth were denied access to this small oasis of safety.

After Stonewall, the worries about this stereotype of the predator were confirmed when the first wave of homophobic reaction to gay liberation framed the issue as a campaign to "Save Our Children" from the sexual perverts who would corrupt them. There were a few cases in the 1970s of school teachers coming out and

Research for this essay is based on the Gay, Lesbian, and Straight Teachers Network Chicago Records and the Patricia Tomaso Papers, Gerber/Hart Library and Archives.

fighting to keep their jobs. Occasionally a high school student, like Aaron Fricke of Rhode Island, asserted the right to be openly gay. And there was a flood of activism among college students who had just reached the so-called age of consent. But, for the most part, youth remained marginal to movement activism and organizational resources. It was not until the 1990s—in the era that produced an organization like BEHIV—that this began to change significantly, and then it did so in an avalanche of activism and organizing.

Two collections at the Gerber/Hart Library and Archives—the papers of GLSTN, the Gay, Lesbian, and Straight Teachers Network (it soon became GLSEN, the Gay, Lesbian, Straight Education Network) and of Patricia Tomaso, a teacher-activist—provide a vivid picture of the explosive growth of organizing around schools and youth. The Chicago chapter was formed in January 1995 by a small group of teachers—Matt Stuczynski, Torey Wilson, and Patricia Tomaso among them. Just fifteen months later, the chapter was hosting a Midwest conference for teachers and educators that brought together three hundred attendees from fourteen states. The size and geographic reach spoke to the need that GLSEN was addressing. Kevin Jennings, the founder and executive director of the national GLSEN, wrote the Chicago cochairs that "your organizational development is astounding . . . you were worried about finding money for stamps this time last year!" An attendee wrote that the conference "felt like the birth of a movement."

In Chicago, the chapter kept busy. From the beginning, it saw its mission as threefold: community organizing, advocacy, and in-school programming. It hosted monthly public programs. It began holding youth summits that brought together students from area schools and trained them in activism. It sent speakers to schools throughout the Chicago area to speak about homophobia in education and what needed to be done. It supported students who wished to organize a Gay-Straight Alliance in their school. It organized contingents of teachers and of youth to march in the annual Pride Parade, thus giving greater visibility to school issues and the needs of youth. At a street fair on Halsted Street, it got over two thousand patrons to sign and send postcards to high school principals. Just three years after its founding, over two hundred teachers were members.

It did not take long for signs to materialize of substantial institutional progress. Patricia Tomaso, who retired as a teacher in 1994 and then promptly came out, played a key role in pushing both the Chicago Teachers Union and the Chicago Public Schools to be more responsive to LGBTQ needs. Late in 1994, she had written to Thomas Reece, president of CTU, explaining how the fear of losing her job had kept her in the closet for decades. She urged Reece to press for a nondiscrimination clause in its employment contract with CPS, and in 1996, such a clause was added. Meanwhile, GLSEN Chicago leaders worked with liaisons in city government to make the powerful documentary film *It's Elementary* available to all of Chicago's public schools. Tennis icon Billie Jean King provided funding so that the film could be widely distributed among schools. Before long, social workers, support staff, and others were attending viewings and engaging in group discussion of the issues. *It's Elementary* proved to be an effective organizing tool. By 1998, the CTU had a Human Rights Subcommittee on Gay and Lesbian Issues that was meeting regularly.

While deeply engaged with Chicago and its environs, the Chicago chapter also kept track of what was happening elsewhere and reported on it to its members. School-based activism was spreading rapidly. Teachers were coming out, students were forming GSAs, and opponents were organizing against it all. Battles of significance were occurring in many places in the second half of the 1990s. In Utah in 1996, a teacher named Clayton Vetter came out on national television, provoking the Utah state legislature to ban all extracurricular activities rather than have to tolerate GSAs. In Arizona, a legislator compared allowing GSAs in the schools to permitting Playboy Clubs as support for heterosexuals. In Plymouth, Michigan, in 1999, there was a battle over the removal of a gay history display in a public school. Until 1999, Eau Claire, Wisconsin, banned LGBTQ-themed books in its schools. The GLSEN newsletter reported on these and other battles, and both national GLSEN and local chapters actively fought back.

The growth of GLSEN was impressive. In the space of just three years, from 1995 to 1998, the number of chapters almost tripled to eighty. In 1999, 750 people attended its national conference in Atlanta. In alternate years, several regional conferences were held as well. Looking at the work of GLSEN Chicago and members such as Tomaso is a useful corrective to the national queer imaginary that makes marriage the overriding issue of the last two decades. Through the initiatives of GLSEN activists, we can see just how much on-the-ground organizing was going on in schools and local communities across the United States and how youth were coming out in impressive numbers.

As often happens, browsing through these archival collections frequently brings up something that elicits surprise or shock or a big smile. In this case, it was a smile. One of GLSEN Chicago's signature events in these years was an annual prom. Named the "Prom You Always Wanted," it was meant for adult same-sex couples who had not been able to go to their prom as part of a same-sex couple when they were in high school. It is not hard to imagine the pleasure it brought to those couples who attended.

38

We Will Not Stay Quiet: The 85% Coalition

Direct-action protest has long been a key feature of movements for social justice. Woman's suffrage, labor union organizing, the black freedom struggle in its many phases, and the opposition of pacifists to war and militarization have all had periods in which activists staged protests designed to block the routine operations of the institutions of power. In the current century, Occupy Wall Street, Black Lives Matter, and the #MeToo movement have all continued the tradition of vocal, disruptive protest.

At various points, direct action has also been a significant part of the LGBTQ movement. In the wake of the police raid on the Stonewall Inn in New York in 1969, street riots occurred for several days. The gay liberation and lesbian-feminist movements that coalesced in the months afterward and that grew rapidly in the early 1970s made militant protest a key tactic. These protests did not simply disrupt; they also brought much-needed visibility and media attention to this new wave of activism. A decade and a half later, as the AIDS epidemic spread and took so many lives, another period of angry protest erupted. Across the country, chapters of ACT UP, the AIDS Coalition to Unleash Power, took to the streets, invaded government buildings, and stopped rush hour traffic as a means of forcing gov-

Research for this essay is based on the 85% Coalition Records, Gerber/Hart Library and Archives.

ernment institutions to address the needs of those with AIDS and adopt policies to fight the epidemic.

In the current century, for the most part, LGBTQ activists have not adopted such tactics in large numbers. Instead, movement organizations have worked through the courts, lobbied elected officials, engaged in voter mobilization, and built community institutions as ways of making change. But while there has been no broad-based direct-action component of the LGBTQ movement in the last two decades, occasionally a group surfaces and inserts disruptive protest into the local struggle against homophobia and LGBTQ oppression.

One such organization was the 85% Coalition. The group was formed in the central Illinois community of Urbana by two lesbian activists, Mary Lee Sargent and Kimberlie Kranich, in November 1999. The name derived from a statewide survey done in the previous year that found that 85% of Illinois voters approved of outlawing discrimination based on sexual orientation. Yet, despite this clear indication of voter opinion, state legislators had failed for more than twenty years to pass such a law. In the fall of 1999, when Kranich and Sargent formed the coalition, an antidiscrimination bill had been introduced yet again into the state assembly, but legislative leaders seemed reluctant to bring it up for a vote.

The papers of the 85% Coalition at the Gerber/Hart Library provide a vivid picture of the group's activities over a period of about five years. Their first demonstrations, held outside the state legislature in November and December 1999, were small but lively. Participants carried a large banner that proclaimed "Heterosexual Rights for Gays," and they chanted and sang as legislators arrived for the day's work. "Every visibility makes a difference," one of the demonstrators told a reporter. Sargent argued that the repeated willingness of legislators to stall had created "a need to add direct action to get more notice."

Over the next handful of years, this small group of activists, almost all of whom were women, reappeared at the state capitol many times to push for hearings and a vote on antidiscrimination bills that sponsors kept introducing. As they gained more experience, they were willing to engage in actions that were more disruptive. In May 2001, they interrupted a senate committee session after the chair of the committee announced that he would not hold hearings on a bill that had been passed by the house. Kranich, Sargent, and three other women stood up, linked hands, and began chanting "No, no, we won't go. We're your daughters, we're your sons, pass House Bill 101." Police forcibly dragged them from the committee room and arrested them on charges of disorderly conduct and disrupting state government proceedings. But the arrests did not quiet them. "We will not be frightened," the coalition announced in a statement it made to the press soon afterward.

The arrests succeeded in gaining a lot of attention, and they provoked a range of reactions. The *News-Gazette*, a central Illinois paper, covered the coalition's actions frequently, usually sympathetically. Jesse White, the Illinois secretary of state, responded by proposing a revision of the state's administrative code so that any group that was arrested because of a protest would be denied future permission to protest in or near government buildings. The coalition engaged the assistance of the Illinois ACLU to fight White's proposal, and he dropped it. But some activists were displeased as well. Rick Garcia, who was the political director for Equality Illinois, the LGBTQ organization that lobbied state legislators, told reporters after the arrests that "I don't think what those folks did today was helpful." Still, Kranich was uncompromising in her response. "This is too important to go quietly," she informed reporters.

All of the arrestees were acquitted when their case came to trial in August, and they almost immediately returned to action. The coalition held a series of public meetings in central Illinois to get their message out and gain more support for their tactics. They showed up at community events held by Republican legislators who were against passage of an antidiscrimination bill. They conducted a "sing-in" at the office of Rick Winkel, a Republican state senator who was on record as opposed to antidiscrimination legislation. In May 2002, on the anniversary of their arrest the previous year, they were back in Springfield, the state capital. From the gallery of the state senate, they hung a huge banner that called out Pate Phillips, the president of the senate, who had been forthright in his opposition to these bills. Coalition members began singing:

> Glory, glory hallelujah, equal rights are comin' to ya,
> It's time to stop the hate, let us not discriminate,
> Gay rights in Illinois

When the police came to intervene, the protesters chose to leave rather than get arrested again.

In the public face they presented through their actions, coalition leaders maintained a militant posture. "Social change doesn't happen by asking," Kranich declared to a journalist. Yet, at the same time, the activists in the 85% Coalition were not under the illusion that demonstrations and disruptions by themselves would lead to enactment of an antidiscrimination law. As Meg Miner, one of the leaders of the coalition, told a reporter, "We can't influence the legislators, but we can influence the people who vote for them by getting our cause media coverage."

Soon after the spring 2002 demonstrations, the coalition was presented with a case that brought a compelling personal face to the need for antidiscrimination legislation. Late in May, Lynn Sprout was fired from her job as a pediatric nurse and manager at Carle Foundation Hospital in Urbana. The previous year, Sprout had begun taking time off in order to care for her partner, Linda Schurvinske, who was suffering from advanced cirrhosis of the liver. The hospital did not recognize same-sex partners as family, and so Sprout could not apply for family medical leave. Coworkers began donating their vacation time so that she could remain at home. After her partner passed away and Sprout returned to work, she noticed a change in her treatment. Despite having worked at Carle for fifteen years and having the respect of those she worked with, her supervisor told her that "you are just not the right mix" for the hospital. "We prefer that you do not work anywhere at Carle," and she found herself terminated.

Fortunately for Sprout, the town of Urbana had passed an ordinance banning discrimination based on sexual orientation. But the Human Relations Commission had never ruled on such a case before, and it took two years before it finally scheduled hearings on the complaint. In the meantime, the 85% Coalition did everything it could to keep Sprout's case in the public eye and to pressure the Human Relations Commission to act. Members and supporters lined the main streets of Urbana with signs backing Sprout. Urbana's public television station covered the demonstrations. Kranich sent a stream of emails urging their followers to act. "By coming out like fire and showing that the public supports Lynn, we are putting pressure on Carle Hospital," she wrote. "They hate the publicity." Activists from the 85% Coalition showed up in large numbers at the hearings, so that the Human Relations Commission would know that it was under scrutiny.

In November 2004, the commission finally ruled in favor of Sprout. In April 2005, Carle Foundation Hospital reached a confidential settlement with her. It also agreed to change its policies to grant employees in same-sex domestic partnerships (marriage equality had not yet come to Illinois) both family medical leave in case of illness and bereavement leave when a partner passed away. Carle's intention to appeal the decision and its hard-line resistance likely finally collapsed because of a momentous event that occurred in the midst of these hearings and negotiations. In January 2005, the Illinois state legislature finally passed a bill prohibiting discrimination based on sexual orientation, and Governor Rod Blagojevich signed it into law. Five years after its founding, the 85% Coalition could rightly claim that its main goal had been realized.

Although the coalition disbanded, many of its core activists continued to fight for equality, but in a new organization. The Sprout case had exposed the cost to same-sex couples of not having their relationships legally recognized, while the achievement of marriage equality in Massachusetts in May 2004—the first state to do this— made marriage seem like an attainable goal. And so, that spring, Kranich and several others formed C-U at the Altar, a Champaign-

Urbana organization committed to achieving marriage equality. That summer, it worked with Lambda Legal, which was supporting a court challenge to achieve marriage equality, to organize a central Illinois Marriage Equality Bus Tour. "We are writing sketches to be performed during the bus tour," one member wrote to the group's email list. "The goal is to provoke conversation about gay marriage and educate about the differences between civil marriage and civil unions." The bus made stops at farmers markets, street fairs, shopping malls, and campuses to educate people about the need for marriage equality.

The coalition papers, which end in 2005, do not reveal how long C-U at the Altar lasted, nor what it continued to do in the months and years after Governor Blagojevich signed the antidiscrimination bill into law. Nor can the documents resolve the question of how much the direct-action tactics of the group contributed to its final passage. Kranich remained a firm believer in the value of the coalition's work. "I believe that any change requires a movement and a grassroots effort," she told the *News-Gazette* after the senate approved the bill. "You need direct action, you need people to get arrested, you need people to lobby, and that's what ultimately after 30 years, allowed this bill to be passed." Other research, in the papers of state legislators and of more traditional lobbying organizations, would bring more evidence to bear on the impact of the 85% Coalition. One can say with certainty, however, that coalition activists did bring media attention to the issue and raised the level of public awareness in central Illinois during these years. And, whether effective or not, one cannot help but admire the courage, determination, and daring of this small group of activists who refused to accept, in the opening years of the twenty-first century, the disregard of elected officials for the needs of the LGBTQ community.

Afterword: Further Reading

As I mentioned in the introduction to this collection of essays, I do not claim to cover the vast expanse of Chicago's LGBTQ history since the 1960s. Rather, each essay tells a story that offers a particular vantage point on this history. Through the lives of some individuals, through the work of particular organizations with a focused mission, through events that had an impact on many people's lives, I hope that you, the reader, appreciate how rich, varied, and complex that history is.

At the same time, I hope that, taken together, these essays point to certain insights. First and most obviously perhaps, individuals make a difference. Whether it is Renee Hanover using her legal skills, or the journalistic reporting of George Buse, or the impulsive political campaign of Gary Nepon, or the compelling stage performances of Robinn Dupree, individuals have an impact that reaches beyond their own lives and those closest to them.

Another conclusion to be drawn from these stories of Chicago's LGBTQ past is that when individuals do come together to work collectively, their power and influence are magnified enormously. Over the course of two decades, the women of Amigas Latinas were able to do far more to change the public face of LGBTQ Chicago than any single individual could have accomplished. The massive, visible voter registration drive of the Impact '88 campaign shifted dramatically the stance that the city's legislative body took in relation to the LGBTQ community and hastened passage of nondiscrimination legislation. Through the work of an organization like GLAAD, media coverage of the community shifted in the 1990s.

A number of the essays highlight the ways that cultural production and social activity can be community-building devices that strengthen a collective identity and hence provide a more solid foundation for political mobilization. Groups like Frontrunners and the Metropolitan Sports Association not only provided opportunities for LGBTQ individuals to have fun together; they also created greater visibility in Chicago and raised money that helped important community organizations fulfill their missions. The women of Metis Press brought lesbian writing into print at a time when commercial publishers had no interest in such work; their success helped open up the mainstream industry. Begun as a social club to create a space for interracial dating, Black and White Men Together became a force in the fight against AIDS. Examples like these could be multiplied across the last half century of LGBTQ history.

Finally, though the topics covered by these essays range broadly, one might argue that what links them all is the reality of a growing LGBTQ movement from the 1960s to the present. The lives of Merle Markland and George Buse could change so profoundly because an organized movement had helped to create a visible out-of-the-closet community with institutions that brought people together openly. The women forming Artemis Singers loved music, but they were motivated to form Artemis by the changes that an organized lesbian-feminist movement had achieved in the 1970s, and they saw their performances as agents of further change. The lawyers who gathered together at a national conference in Chicago in 1987 to evaluate the state of the law and plan strategies for the future recognized themselves as part of a larger mobilization to reform the law and public policy. The organizations that proliferated in and helped to solidify a diverse LGBTQ community since the 1960s had wildly different emphases—police behavior, law reform, musical production, voter mobilization, athletics, school curriculum. But cumulatively they shared the desire to create a society in which LGBTQ people might live free from stigma and oppression.

In that shared wish, they all contributed to building a movement whose influence has been felt widely and whose achievements have been consequential.

I also hope that these travels into Chicago's LGBTQ past have highlighted how important the project of saving and preserving the documents of the past is. Without the archiving of history, the writing of history cannot be done, and the capacity to learn from the past—whether those lessons be sobering or inspiring—will be fatally compromised. This is especially true for LGBTQ history. Every essay in this book had its origins in an archival collection at the Gerber/Hart Library and Archives. The creation of community-based archives since the 1970s has been another component of the multifaceted LGBTQ movement. The stories I have told in these pages are not those of the rich, famous, and powerful—the individuals who are stereotypically considered important enough to have their papers preserved and archived. The growing body of LGBTQ history that has been published in the last three decades has been possible in large part because of the existence of places like Gerber/Hart in cities across the United States. And organizations like Gerber/Hart in Chicago, the Lesbian Herstory Archives in Brooklyn, the Stonewall Archives in Fort Lauderdale, the GLBT Historical Society in San Francisco, and many more are welcoming sites for anyone who wishes to learn more of this history and who wants to experience the excitement of discovery that I have tried to communicate through the writing of these stories.

While there is much LGBTQ history still waiting to be researched and written, there is also much that has already appeared in print. If these essays have aroused your curiosity to learn more, here are some suggestions for further reading.

A number of books provide an overview of LGBTQ history in the United States, among them Leila Rupp, *A Desired Past: A Short History of Same-Sex Love in America*; Michael Bronski, *A Queer History of the United States*; and Susan Stryker, *Transgender History*. Stephen Angelides provides an overview of the role and meaning of the concept of bisexuality in *The History of Bisexuality*. And the founding text of LGBTQ history—Jonathan Ned Katz's *Gay American History: Lesbians and Gay Men in the U.S.A.*—provides hundreds of pages of documents stretching back to the early seventeenth century, documents that, despite the book's subtitle, reach beyond lesbian and gay to provide evidence of transgender and bisexual lives in the nation's past.

There is also a growing literature specifically about the history of Chicago. St. Sukie De la Croix offers a sweeping view, grounded in documents, of the century before the emergence of gay liberation at the end of the 1960s in *Chicago Whispers: A History of LGBT Chicago before Stonewall.* Timothy Stewart-Winter has published a history of LGBTQ activism in Chicago from the 1950s into the early 1990s: *Queer Clout: Chicago and the Rise of Gay Politics.* Two edited collections of essays survey a range of topics: *Out and Proud in Chicago: An Overview of the City's Gay Community*, edited by Tracy Baim; and *Out in Chicago: LGBT History at the Crossroads*, edited by Jill Austin and Jennifer Brier. The Austin and Brier anthology grew out of a major exhibit that was on display at the Chicago History Museum in 2011 and 2012.

Readers interested in getting a deeper sense of the history related to specific essays might wish to explore some of the following books. David K. Johnson's *The Lavender Scare* and Douglas M. Charles's *Hoover's War on Gays* provide a sense of how oppressive the decades of the 1950s and 1960s were, such that people like Merle Markham and George Buse remained in the closet. An earlier book of mine, *Sexual Politics, Sexual Communities*, describes the activism of the pre-Stonewall years when Renee Hanover was beginning to take on LGBTQ-related legal cases. In their biography *Jim Flint: The Boy from Peoria*, Tracy Baim and Owen Keehnen write at length about the bar, the Baton, where Robinn Dupree got her start as a performer.

Stonewall ushered in a new, more militant era of activism. Two books from the early years of gay liberation—*Out of the Closets*, edited by Karla Jay and Allen Young, and *The Gay Militants*, by Donn Teal—capture the passion and excitement that erupted in the wake of Stonewall and the birth of a liberation movement. More recently, in *The Stonewall Riots*, Marc Stein has brought together a rich collection of documents related to this decisive moment, while Jim Downs explores some of the key episodes of the 1970s in *Stand by Me*. Two recent books offer broad overviews of the history of LGBTQ activism across the last half century: Marc Stein, *Rethinking the Gay and Lesbian Movement*, and Lillian Faderman, *The Gay Revolution*.

Book-length studies exist for some of the topical areas covered in individual essays. In *Reforming Sodom: Protestants and the Rise of Gay Rights*, Heather R. White offers a big-picture view of how a large segment of American religious communities grappled with the emergence of activism around sexual identities. The historical role of the law in the oppression of LGBTQ people and how that changed in the face of activism is the focus of two books by William N. Eskridge: *Gaylaw: Challenging the Apartheid of the Closet* and *Dishonorable Passions: Sodomy Laws in America*. In *Rainbow Rights*, Patricia Cain focuses on the role of lawyers in the struggle for equality. Amin Ghaziani provides an insightful account of the Marches on Washington that activists organized, including the 1987 March on Washington, in *The Dividends of Dissent*.

The historical writing on lesbian activism, social life, and culture is extensive. Marcia Gallo offers an account of lesbian activism in the 1950s and 1960s in *Different Daughters*, a history of the Daughters of Bilitis, a pioneering lesbian rights organization. Jeannette Foster's classic work *Sex Variant Women in Literature* served as an inspiration for the women, like those of Metis Press, who built a lesbian-feminist publishing world in the 1970s and 1980s. In *The Feminist Bookstore Movement*, Kristen Hogan looks at the role that lesbians played in sustaining an alternative culture of books. The world of women's music festivals, in which the Artemis Singers participated, is the subject of a book by Bonnie J. Morris, *Eden Built by Eves*. And Arlene Stein offers an overview of lesbian-feminist consciousness and political outlook in the decades after Stonewall and the rise of second-wave feminism in *Sex and Sensibility: Stories of a Lesbian Generation*.

African American gay activism is the subject of Kevin Mumford's book *Not Straight, Not White: Black Gay Men from the March on Washington to the AIDS Crisis*. Cathy Cohen delves into the impact that the AIDS epidemic had on African American activism more broadly in *The Boundaries of Blackness*. The literature on the AIDS epidemic, including its history, is vast. John-Manuel Andriote provides an overview of the impact of AIDS on gay male life in *Victory Deferred*, while Jennifer Brier provides an in-depth look at the political responses to AIDS in *Infectious Ideas*, and Anthony Petro examines the response of religious communities to the epidemic in *After the Wrath of God*.

A growing number of books cover aspects of LGBTQ history that are relevant to the chapters that cover the 1990s and the early twenty-first century. In *Up from Invisibility*, Larry Gross explores the way media covered LGBTQ issues and how organizations like GLAAD responded. A. Finn Enke discusses the role of sports in building community among lesbians in *Finding the Movement*, while Steve Estes offers insight into the experience of military service in *Ask and Tell: Gay and Lesbian Veterans Speak Out*. Jackie Blount investigates the issue of schools and the struggle of LGBTQ teachers across the twentieth century in *Fit to Teach*. And *Queer Brown Voices*, edited by Uriel Quesada, Letitia Gomez, and Salvador Vidal-Ortiz, puts the work of Amigas Latinas into a broad context of Latinx LGBTQ activism.

Acknowledgments

In my experience, writing a book only happens with the support and assistance of others. In this case, I would like to express my deepest thanks to the Gerber/Hart Library and Archives of Chicago, without which this book would have been impossible. I have dedicated the volume to the memory of Gregory Sprague, who, in the late 1970s and early 1980s, did the work that led to Gerber/Hart's founding and to the inclusion of archiving as an essential part of its mission. I knew Greg in these years, when a small number of us scattered around the US were initiating the work of uncovering and producing an LGBTQ history. Greg was also one of the founders in 1978 of the Committee on Lesbian and Gay History of the American Historical Association (now the Committee on Lesbian, Gay, Bisexual, and Transgender History), which has played a major role in moving the work of LGBTQ history forward and establishing a recognized place for it within the historical profession. Sadly, Greg was one of the many casualties of the AIDS epidemic and did not live to see the flourishing of this new field of history.

I also want to thank Carrie Barnett, a former board president of Gerber/Hart, and Wil Brant, its current director. All community-based organizations experience highs and lows, and Gerber/Hart is no exception. Both Carrie and Wil, each in different ways, have made huge contributions toward making these last few years one of the best periods in Gerber/Hart's history. As both library and archive, it is functioning exceedingly well, and its community programming is more extensive than ever. With regard to the archives, Alyssa Sadusky has played a critical role in supervising the processing of collections, and the various archival collections are now more accessible to researchers than ever before.

This book had its beginnings as a series of blog posts on the website Outhistory.org, of which I have been a codirector for a number of years. I want to thank my dear friend Jonathan Ned Katz, the creator of Outhistory, as well as Claire Bond Potter, another codirector, who encouraged the development of the "In the Archives" series of blog posts. After doing a few posts, I realized that, rather than producing a continuous narrative history of Chicago's queer past, a series of separate, though related, essays could constitute a book.

The University of Chicago Press has once again proven itself a pleasure to work with. Doug Mitchell, with whom I worked for forty years, displayed an interest in this project from our first discussion of it and acquired it for the press. After Doug retired, Timothy Mennel took charge of it and has been very accessible and supportive throughout. The readers Timothy solicited to evaluate the manuscript offered constructive suggestions about the structure and direction of the project. Sadly, Doug Mitchell passed away in 2019 and did not live to see this manuscript published. He was an extraordinarily positive force in the development of LGBTQ history and sociology as a field of scholarship. I and many others miss his presence.

Finally, I would like to thank Hal Watkins. He has listened to more of my mumblings on the ups and downs of this project than anyone ought to be subjected to. But his smile and support remained consistent throughout, and he kept me going in more ways than he probably realizes.

Bibliography

Andriote, John-Manuel. *Victory Deferred: How AIDS Changed Gay Life in America*. Chicago: University of Chicago Press, 1999.

Angelides, Stephen. *The History of Bisexuality*. Chicago: University of Chicago Press, 2001.

Austin, Jill, and Jennifer Brier, eds. *Out in Chicago: LGBT History at the Crossroads*. Chicago: Chicago History Museum, 2011.

Baim, Tracy, ed. *Out and Proud in Chicago: An Overview of the City's Gay Community*. Chicago: Surrey Books, 2008.

Baim, Tracy, and Owen Keehnen. *Jim Flint: The Boy from Peoria*. Chicago: Prairie Avenue Productions, 2011.

Blount, Jackie M. *Fit to Teach: Same-Sex Desire, Gender, and School Work in the Twentieth Century*. Albany: State University of New York Press, 2005.

Brier, Jennifer. *Infectious Ideas: U.S. Political Responses to the AIDS Crisis*. Chapel Hill: University of North Carolina Press, 2009.

Bronski, Michael. *A Queer History of the United States*. Boston: Beacon Press, 2011.

Cain, Patricia. *Rainbow Rights: The Role of Lawyers and Courts in the Lesbian and Gay Civil Rights Movement*. Boulder, CO: Westview Press, 2000.

Charles, Douglas M. *Hoover's War on Gays: Exposing the FBI's "Sex Deviates" Program*. Lawrence: University of Kansas Press, 2015.

Cohen, Cathy J. *The Boundaries of Blackness: AIDS and the Breakdown of Black Politics*. Chicago: University of Chicago Press, 1999.

De La Croix, St. Sukie. *Chicago Whispers: A History of LGBT Chicago before Stonewall*. Madison: University of Wisconsin Press, 2012.

D'Emilio, John. *Sexual Politics, Sexual Communities: The Making of a Homosexual Minority in the United States, 1940–1970*. Chicago: University of Chicago Press, 1983; 2nd edition, 1998.

Downs, Jim. *Stand by Me: The Forgotten History of Gay Liberation*. New York: Basic Books, 2016.

Enke, Anne. *Finding the Movement: Sexuality, Contested Space, and Feminist Activism*. Durham, NC: Duke University Press, 2007.

Eskridge, William N. *Dishonorable Passions: Sodomy Laws in America, 1861–2003*. New York: Viking Press, 2008.

Eskridge, William N. *Gaylaw: Challenging the Apartheid of the Closet*. Cambridge, MA: Harvard University Press, 1999.

Estes, Steve. *Ask and Tell: Gay and Lesbian Veterans Speak Out*. Chapel Hill: University of North Carolina Press, 2007.

Faderman, Lillian. *The Gay Revolution: The Story of the Struggle*. New York: Simon and Schuster, 2015.

Foster, Jeannette. *Sex Variant Women in Literature*. Baltimore: Diana Press, 1975.

Gallo, Marcia. *Different Daughters: A History of the Daughters of Bilitis and the Rise of the Lesbian Rights Movement*. New York: Carroll and Graf, 2006.

Ghaziani, Amin. *The Dividends of Dissent: How Conflict and Culture Work in Lesbian and Gay Marches on Washington*. Chicago: University of Chicago Press, 2008.

Gross, Larry. *Up from Invisibility: Lesbians, Gay Men, and the Media in America*. New York: Columbia University Press, 2001.

Hogan, Kristen. *The Feminist Bookstore Movement: Lesbian Antiracism and Feminist Accountability*. Durham, NC: Duke University Press, 2016.

Jay, Karla, and Allen Young. *Out of the Closets: Voices of Gay Liberation*. New York: New York University Press, 1992.

Johnson, David K. *The Lavender Scare: The Cold War Persecutions of Gays and Lesbians in the Federal Government*. Chicago: University of Chicago Press, 2004.

Katz, Jonathan Ned. *Gay American History: Lesbians and Gay Men in the U.S.A.* New York: Thomas Crowell, 1976.

Morris, Bonnie J. *Eden Built by Eves: The Culture of Women's Music Festivals.* Los Angeles: Alyson Books, 1999.

Mumford, Kevin J. *Not Straight, Not White: Black Gay Men from the March on Washington to the AIDS Crisis.* Chapel Hill: University of North Carolina Press, 2016.

Petro, Anthony M. *After the Wrath of God: AIDS, Sexuality and American Religion.* New York: Oxford University Press, 2015.

Quesada, Uriel, Letitia Gomez, and Salvador Vidal-Ortiz, eds. *Queer Brown Voices: Personal Narratives of Latina/o LGBT Activism.* Austin: University of Texas Press, 2015.

Rupp, Leila J. *A Desired Past: A Short History of Same-Sex Love in America.* Chicago: University of Chicago Press, 1999.

Stein, Arlene. *Sex and Sensibility: Stories of a Lesbian Generation.* Berkeley: University of California Press, 1997.

Stein, Marc. *Rethinking the Gay and Lesbian Movement.* New York: Routledge, 2012.

Stein, Marc. *The Stonewall Riots: A Documentary History.* New York: New York University Press, 2019.

Stewart-Winter, Timothy. *Queer Clout: Chicago and the Rise of Gay Politics.* Philadelphia: University of Pennsylvania Press, 2016.

Stryker, Susan. *Transgender History.* Berkeley, CA: Seal Press, 2008.

Teal, Donn. *The Gay Militants: How Gay Liberation Began in America, 1969–1971.* New York: St. Martin's Press, 1995.

White, Heather R. *Reforming Sodom: Protestants and the Rise of Gay Rights.* Chapel Hill: University of North Carolina Press, 2015.

Index